What God Starts, God Completes

I0894392

Michael A. Milton

From my youth I have sung, 'I love to tell the story to those who know it best [and] seem hungering and thirsting to hear it like the rest.' Those who know the gospel of Jesus Christ's saving love never tire of its themes and delight to hear them sung again in the lives of his children. Pastor Mike Milton knows the tune well because it has been sung so beautifully in his life. May this story of salvation bring praise again to our Savior and bring delight to those yet hungering and thirsting to be filled with the goodness of his grace.

Dr. Bryan Chapell,
Chancellor, Covenant Theological Seminary, St Louis, Missouri

In this book you will read the account of a man who has been saved by the Gospel of Jesus Christ, set aside to serve Christ and thus an instrument of God to extend the glory of God and expand the Kingdom of God all by the power of God. Mike Milton's life unfolded in such an intriguing and interesting manner in this volume reminds us that to be Gospel-saved is to be Gospel-driven and even more importantly to be captured by the love of Christ. Enjoy this page-turner and remember that this same Christ can be yours and you can be His.

Dr. Harry L. Reeder, III,
Pastor, Briarwood Presbyterian Church, Birmingham, Alabama

The Rev. Dr. Mike Milton is a godly, zealous pastor and also a trophy of God's sovereign, amazing love in Christ. I welcome this new book by him for at least two reasons. First and foremost, it glorifies the Triune God. Second, its warm, humble and personalized approach makes it extremely attractive and readable. Read it and give copies to your friends. This book will help them.

Rev. Dr. D. Eryl Davies,
Head of Research & Principal Emeritus,
Wales Evangelical School of Theology, Brigend, Wales

A true pastor reaches to the heart. Mike Milton is such a pastor. Because God has radically changed his heart, he longs to speak to the hearts of others about God's amazing grace. His open heart will touch yours, too.

Robert C. (Ric) Cannada, Jr.,
Chancellor Emeritus, Reformed Theological Seminary

In this self-disclosing autobiography, Dr. Mike Milton embraces the paradox of *strength in weakness*. The one who reads this volume runs the risk of finding freedom in captivity to Christ and power in the declaration of dependence on Christ.

Dr. Robert Smith, Jr.,
Assoc Professor, Beeson Divinity School of Samford University, Birmingham, Alabama

As you read Mike Milton's story, you will undoubtedly discover multiple connections with your own life, whatever your age and stage. This means that the grace that God has displayed throughout his story can be displayed in yours as well. As a college president, I'm particularly hopeful that this book will help rising generations establish the biblical, joyful perspective of God's providence as they prepare for the pathways of God's calling. Don't miss this encouraging invitation to 'taste and see that the Lord is good.'

Dr. Niel Nielson,
President, Maclellan Center for Global Christian Education,
Lookout Mountain, Georgia

Mike Milton's story of God's amazing grace in his life is powerful. I have shared his story with others ever since I heard it several years ago. I am so glad it is now in print. Don't miss this one!

Dr. Frank M. Barker, Jr.,
Pastor Emeritus, Briarwood Presbyterian Church, Birmingham, Alabama

I commend this Mike Milton life story! It's a story of God's amazing grace, fleshed out in Mike's unique life experiences. His writing style is edgy and his ultimate message profound! I find it interesting, insightful and challenging!

Dr. John Huffman,
Chairman of the Board, Christianity Today

Mike Milton has taken the risk to tell us his story, all of it. The parable of his life, like yours and mine, was composed by the Creator and is only understandable in His light.It is a story of grace, gracefully told.

Michael Card,
Singer/Musician

All grace is 'Amazing Grace'. For some of us, who are converted early in life, God saves us from what we would have become without Christ. For others, such as Mike Milton, who are born again after years of life apart from Christ, God in his sovereign grace, rescues from the ravages of the Destroyer, relieves the misery of sin, removes the burden of guilt and grants a new quality of life as well as life eternal.

Dr. L. Roy Taylor,
Stated Clerk of the General Assembly of the Presbyterian Church in America

God's amazing grace in the lives of his saints is inspiring and this biography is another chapter in God's grand narrative, a chapter well worth reading.

Dr. Luder G. Whitlock, Jr,
Executive Director of CNL Charitable Foundation

I have been a friend and worked professionally with Dr. Michael Milton for nearly fifteen years. While Mike's life story is without doubt inspirational, it is also a lifeline of encouragement to those who are struggling through their own stormy trials of life. *What God Starts, God Completes* will re-energize your heart as to the grace of our heavenly Father in your life as you read the story of God's remarkable work which began in an abandoned five year old little boy named Mike, who literally had nothing other than the prayers of a faithful and loving aunt.

J. Thomas Lamprecht,
President, Atlantic Coast Communications

The transforming power of the Gospel is the Good News Christians herald to needy people broken by sin. Dr. Mike Milton in this autobiography powerfully combines his own story of Gospel restoration with a compelling invitation to trust in the One who loved us and gave Himself for us in our brokenness, Jesus Christ.

Jim Bland,
Coordinator, Mission to North America, Presbyterian Church in America

Michael Milton's biography of how God drew him to a living faith is an encourage-ment to every believer, that God can save those from the 'guttermost' to the 'uttermost.' I am honored to call him my friend and hero.

Rev. Dr. John Guest,
Pastor Emeritus of Christ Church and Pastor of the Chapel at Ocean Reed,
Key Largo, Florida

I'm always refreshed and encouraged when I hear Mike Milton speak. He speaks about God from experience. His life story includes pain, difficulty, mistakes and sins. Given his life you get the impression that he thinks it is just too good to be true that the Creator of the universe really loves him. But he's utterly convinced that He does. That's why I like to hear him speak. If it's true for Mike just maybe I've got hope too.

Rev. Ron Brown,
Campus Minister, Covenant College, Lookout Mountain, Georgia

Get ready for an inspiring story! You are about to read of a life that has experienced the transforming power of the gospel of Jesus Christ. I am one who has had the privilege of working with and being under the pastoral ministry of Mike Milton. He preaches out of brokenness and knows that he will always have an audience when he preaches to broken people. Give this story to everyone that needs to hear God's promise that He will bring 'to completion' that 'good work' of grace which He begins in His children's life (Phil. 1:6). Give this book to everyone that needs to know that grace can 'restore to you' what seems like a life lost or wasted by the ravages of sin (Joel 2:25). Give this story to everyone who needs to hear of the love of Jesus Christ!

Rev. M. Steve Wallace,
Chief of Staff/COO, Reformed Theological Seminary

Too many 'before and after' testimonies, secular and religious, fail to ring true. The 'before' seems unrealistically *bad*. The 'after' seems unrealistically *good*. The road between the 'before' and 'after' seems unrealistically *easy*. Mike Milton, one of the outstanding Presbyterian ministers in the English-speaking world, has provided us with an inspiring account of his Christian conversion that encourages us simply because it remains anchored to reality.

The 'bad' was really bad: a difficult childhood, rebellious adolescence, self-indulgent young-adulthood. The 'good' has been really good: an encounter with Jesus that rescued him from a futile existence and brought peace, hope, and purpose into his life. Yet from 'before' to 'after' Mike remains Mike, and real: transformed, yet he remains flawed; victorious, yet he suffers defeats; rejoicing, yet not without sorrows; a transcendent purpose for his life, yet not without distractions and inconsistencies. In short, this is a story for sinners, for sinners saved by grace, and sinners who by the grace of Christ are wrestling to become saints. I commend it to you wholeheartedly.

Rev. Terry L. Johnson,
Senior Minister, Independent Presbyterian Church, Savannah, Georgia

What God Starts, God Completes

Gospel hope for hurting people

Third Edition

Michael A. Milton

Christian Focus

To contact Michael Milton for preaching engagements, conferences or musical performances, please visit http://michaelmilton.org at Reformed Theological Seminary; or write lperez@rts.edu. One may also write Michael Milton at:

Office of the Chancellor
2101 Carmel Road
Charlotte, North Carolina
USA.

ISBN 978-1-84550-823-4 (paperback)
ISBN 978-1-78191-106-8 (hardback)

10 9 8 7 6 5 4 3 2 1

Published in 2007
Reprinted 2008 and 2012
by
Christian Focus Publications,
Geanies House, Fearn, Ross-shire,
IV20 1TW, Scotland, UK

www.christianfocus.com

Cover design by Daniel van Straaten

Printed by MPG, Cornwall, England

MIX
Paper from responsible sources
FSC® C018575

Contents

To the glory of God, and for the help of those who would find the new life in Jesus Christ which has been shown to me, I now dedicate this book.

I dedicate this book also in memory of and with eternal appreciation to Aunt Eva, and with all of my love to Mae, John Michael, and all our children, physical and spiritual.

INTRODUCTION

ROBERT C. 'RIC' CANNADA, JR.

I first met Mike Milton while he was serving as the admissions director for Knox Theological Seminary at the Coral Ridge Presbyterian Church in Ft. Lauderdale, FL. Mike told me then a story that he has told me many times since then.

As you will read in his inspiring autobiography, Mike met the Lord in a very real way through the ministry of D. James Kennedy and his Evangelism Explosion training while Mike was living in Louisiana. A few weeks later, still on fire with his new found faith, Mike was visiting my hometown of Jackson, Mississippi, on business. While in Jackson Mike received a phone call telling him to fly immediately from Jackson to Kansas City to be announced as the new district manager in the Midwest for Ashland Chemical Company. Mike called Mae to tell her about the promotion and that he would not be coming directly home as they had planned.

Sitting next to a woman on the plane from Jackson, this new evangelist began to share the gospel with her. She promptly announced that she was a Christian and a member of First Baptist Church in Jackson. She told Mike, however, that a few rows back was a man whom she knew who needed to hear the gospel and pointed out to Mike that there was an empty seat next to this prospective convert. Mike immediately moved to that seat and began a new gospel conversation. After Mike asked the first question or two, the new seatmate responded that he knew the questions Mike was asking, that he was a Christian, and that he was an elder at the First Presbyterian Church in Jackson. Furthermore, he told Mike that he was a good friend of D. James Kennedy and very familiar with the questions and the gospel message that Mike was sharing. Mike and I have had many laughs about that story over the years, since the woman knew the man she had sent Mike to evangelize and they were actually good friends. It was a joke that she from First Baptist had sent Mike to evangelize someone from First Presbyterian.

The man Mike sought to evangelize on that flight was my father, Robert Cannada, Sr. Thus began a long and good relationship between Mike and my family and Reformed Theological Seminary. Dad asked Mike on the plane that day where he was planning to attend church in Kansas City. When Mike responded that he did not know any churches in the area, Dad directed Mike to the Church in Olathe, KS, and to the pastor, Bob Baxter, who became in Mike's words 'his father in the faith'. Dad as a lawyer and a church leader in the PCA had counseled Bob Baxter and that church in some church property matters in previous years and was familiar with the church. God's sovereignty at work on an airplane!

Later when Mike considered where he would attend seminary he contacted my father who was the Chairman of the Board at RTS. At the time, providential circumstances, including a job to help Mike with seminary expenses, led him to Knox Seminary instead of RTS; but Mike was always positive in his relationships with RTS even during those years when he was a student and an employee at Knox. He kept in contact with my father; and also Mike and I struck up a friendship over the years, especially after I came to work for RTS. We first would see each other and visit at conferences where we both were doing seminary recruiting and in later years at other church meetings. As Mike has said often, he didn't come to RTS immediately but he did get here eventually and 'as quickly as he could'.

Our lives have been intertwined for years. I followed and appreciated Mike's ministry and gentle spirit throughout his years after seminary. When we needed a new President at RTS Charlotte, Mike was recommended by a number of friends and he was a natural person for me to consider. Mike would be leading the RTS campus that I had had the privilege to establish. The faculty, staff, and students at RTS Charlotte had all been recruited there by me and were precious to me. I wanted the best for them. I was thrilled when Mike agreed to join us at RTS Charlotte. In fact, I told the Executive Committee of the RTS Board before they interviewed Mike that they were going to be so pleased with him for the Charlotte presidency that they were also going think he could possibly be the next Chancellor of RTS someday.

Well that day finally came. I had made a plan with our Board chairman when I initially accepted the leadership of RTS to retire as Chancellor after the next decade reaffirmation for accreditation in 2012. I hoped, however, that the RTS Board would publicly identify my successor two years before that change so that everyone in the RTS constituency would have time to get used to the new person before he began to lead. This plan has worked well by God's grace and I could not be more pleased that Mike Milton is the next Chancellor of RTS.

Mike is a godly man. Like us all, he is a sinner saved by grace. We all have our faults; but the Lord has refined Mike into a humble, gracious leader who is focused on the gospel and getting people home 'into the arms of Jesus'. He is also a committed husband and father, faithful to his family.

Mike and I have had similar ministry experiences, both serving as church planters (where you have to move furniture and sweep floors among other things) and as senior pastors of large downtown churches with multiple staff and ministries. Mike also has a Ph.D. in theology, the senior academic degree. He is a musician, a creative writer and a military chaplain. In addition, Mike is an excellent communicator in his preaching and teaching as well as in his books and blogs. I know the leadership required in his previous church positions and also as the leader of RTS. Mike has outstanding leadership training and experience in the military and in business as well as in church ministry. All of this background will be needed for his new position, and all of these experiences will help him serve well.

I rejoice in God's goodness to bring Mike Milton to RTS at this time in our history, at this time in the history of our country and the world with so many opportunities for further service and impact. May you be blessed as you read this book and see God's grace preparing Mike for his ministry at RTS and may you be encouraged to see God's goodness in your own life and experiences as well.

Preface

Robert L. Reymond

When my dear and highly-esteemed friend Mike Milton asked me to write a short foreword to his autobiography that celebrates God's gracious transformation of his life from sinner to saint, I agreed to do so without hesitation and with heartfelt alacrity. I will not say anything about this transformation here; he does that well enough and much better than I could do if I were writing his biography. Rather, almost in a 'stream of consciousness' fashion, I will tell you a little about the man I know and simply recount several vignettes that are stamped indelibly in my mind about his days as a student at Knox Theological Seminary and later.

I will always thank God that he led Mike Milton to attend Knox Seminary. Knox Seminary opened its doors in 1990. He was a member of the first graduating class of 1993 and was the second of only two graduating M. Div. students that year; second only because the other graduate's name beginning with 'L' walked across the platform first to receive his degree. Especially am I grateful to Mike for coming to Knox Seminary because he could have gone to virtually any seminary in the country had he chosen to do so, but he chose to attend Knox Seminary. Many people, you know, are happy to climb aboard a bandwagon for the ride after someone else has made it and it is moving (and often they try to take it over when they get there), but Mike came to us when Knox Seminary was little more than a dream. We first faculty members, Dr. George W. Knight, III, Dr. Joseph H. Hall, and I, had promised Mike when he contacted us that we were going to start a Reformed seminary and that he would receive a sound and solid theological education if he came with us. So he came! What a happy union his days with us turned out to be. When one recalls that he moved his family of four (his wife Mae, his aunt Eva, and his step-daughter who attended Westminster Academy) all the way from Kansas to South Florida (Fort Lauderdale) and continued to work full-time as a very successful salesman for Ashland Chemical Company the entire time he was in seminary, it is something of a marvel that he finished as quickly as he did. But Mike completed his studies in three years and did fine academic work for us while he was there. I recall more than once being struck with his diligent labor as he would turn in papers I had assigned him to write even days before they were due. How he managed to do this I will never know.

There was also a joyful, laughing side to Mike during his seminary days. I recall when my systematics class, at his instigation, presented me in class with a pull-over shirt after my lectures on Benjamin B. Warfield's *The Plan of Salvation* that read on the front, 'I am a supernaturalistic, evangelical, particularistic, consistent supralapsarian,' and on the back was the question, 'What are you?' I wore that shirt proudly and often and got a few questions about what it meant from passers-by.

Mike and Mae played the wonderful host and hostess in their home for the small seminary student body on several occasions during those first years. The food was always delicious and presented so invitingly. It was on these occasions that I got to know better Aunt Eva and his step-daughter, although I saw them both regularly in church every Sunday. I remember on one such occasion noticing a map of the starry heavens hanging on his wall in the living room and I asked him about it. Was it celebrating God's handiwork? Was it hanging there because he was an astronomy buff? No, neither of these. Rather, it pinpointed one star in the vast universe that he had paid a company to name for Mae his wife. There is a star somewhere out there today bearing the name of Mae Milton and an arrow on the map pointed it out. So I quickly learned that there was a romantic side to my dear friend as well.

Then there was the time when Hurricane Andrew was bearing down on South Florida and my wife Shirley and I were ordered to evacuate our home and head north and inland. Living where they did, Mike and Mae invited us to ride out the hurricane in their home, which invitation we gladly accepted. I slept that night on their sofa in the family room, and Mike kids me to this day that he was awakened in the middle of the night by a strange noise; I was 'sawing logs' through one of the worst storms ever to hit that part of the state. I remind him just as often that 'a good conscience makes a soft pillow' in the midst of a storm.

It was our joy to return the favor of sharing our home with them when, after his graduation, Mike and Mae returned to Fort Lauderdale when their son, John Michael, was born. They spent the first night of their parenting this little boy in our home, sharing him with us.

Then Mike honored me by asking me to preach his ordination and installation sermon at Redeemer Presbyterian Church (PCA), Overland Park, Kansas. So you can see that there are many things that tie our families together.

But what binds Bob Reymond and Mike Milton together above everything else – above our teacher-student relationship, above the good times we shared together – is the 'common salvation' (Jude 3) we share and our shared love for the Reformed faith. I think I can speak for Mike when I say that the Reformed faith is for both of us a *passion* and a *mission*. We both view the five great *sola's* of the Magisterial Reformation – *Grace* alone, *Christ* alone, *Faith* alone, *Scripture* alone, with our salvation redounding to the *Glory* of God alone – as matters of eternal life and eternal death for the peoples of this world. Agreeing with the Magisterial Reformers, we have both come to understand, by the grace of God, of course, the following truths:

✧ The *only* man with whom the infinitely holy God can have *direct* fellowship is Jesus Christ, the only mediator 'between God and man' (1 Tim. 2:5), and that it is only as sinful people, such as Mike and I, place their trust in Christ's saving cross-work and are thereby regarded by God as no longer 'in Adam' but 'in Christ' that the triune God can have any fellowship with them (this is the *solus Christus* or 'Christ alone' principle of salvation).

✧ The only way to protect the *solus Christus* and the *sola gratia* ('grace alone') of salvation is to insist upon *sola fide* ('faith alone') as the instrumental means of justification, and the only way to protect *sola fide* as the instrumental means of justification is to insist upon the *solus Christus* and the *sola gratia* of salvation.

✧ The only way to protect both the *solus Christus* and the *sola gratia* of salvation and the *sola fide* of justification is to insist upon *sola Scriptura* ('Scripture alone') as the church's sole inspired, inerrant authority in such matters.

✧ Justification by faith is not to be set off over against justification by works as such but over against justification by *our* works, for justification is indeed grounded in Christ's alien preceptive and penal obedience to the Law of God in our stead, whose obedience we receive through faith alone.

- ✧ Saving faith is to be directed solely to the doing and dying of Christ alone and never in any sense to the good works or inner experience of the believer.
- ✧ The Christian's righteousness before God today is *in heaven* at the right hand of God in Jesus Christ and *not on earth* within the believer.
- ✧ The ground of our justification is the vicarious work of Christ *for* us, not the gracious work of the Spirit *in* us.
- ✧ The faith-righteousness of justification is
  - ➢ not personal but vicarious,
  - ➢ not infused but imputed,
  - ➢ not experiential but forensic,
  - ➢ not psychological but legal,
  - ➢ not our own but Christ's alien righteousness, and
  - ➢ not earned but graciously given through faith in Christ, which faith in Christ is itself a gift of grace

We have both learned too that

- ✧ The salvation of the elect is to be credited to God's grace alone (*sola gratia*) to whom alone belongs all the praise for their salvation (*soli Deo gloria*).

It is Mike's story of how he was brought to saving faith in Jesus Christ, how he came to love the Reformed faith, and how he 'left a career to follow a call' that his book tells so personally and sincerely and in such interesting detail. I join with him in prayer that God will use it as an instrument of grace to bring others to Christ, to the Reformed faith, and into the Christian ministry.

Editorial Notes

I have used the English Standard Version of the Holy Bible[1] except where noted. In seeking to present the book in a more conversational way, I have avoided the use of footnotes, though my intentions are most certainly to give credit where, when, and to whom credit is due. I have benefited personally from the sermons, books, and insights of so many. I am sure my own thoughts are so saturated with those of others that it is not only possible but inevitable that I have overlooked giving credit to everyone who deserves it. If anyone sees such an instance, please don't hesitate to let me know, and we will remedy that should there be future editions published.

I do wish to acknowledge the many quotes from Arthur Bennett's now classic *The Valley of Vision: A Collection of Puritan Prayers and Devotions.*[2] The dog-eared pages of my own copy, the frequent underscoring of a phrase or word that

---

[1] *New Reformation Study Bible: English Standard Version,* First ed. (Phillipsburg, NJ: P&R Pub., 2005).

[2] Arthur Bennett, ed., *The Valley of Vision: A Collection of Puritan Prayers and Devotions,* Fifth ed. (Edinburgh: Banner of Truth, 2005).

helped me in thinking through each stage of my testimony, as well as the many quotes themselves, bear witness to my own estimation of the book. I commend it to the reader.

Christian testimonies ought to be about Christ and not primarily about a person. I am sure you agree. But the God who appeared in flesh continues to come to us through flesh – human beings like you and me – bearing witness to His presence and power so that others might be drawn to Him. I hope that I have been faithful to my Lord in such a way that He may use these pages to draw people unto Himself and to bring His healing to His children who suffer from the pain of their past. If any reader feels that this is not so, I ask your forgiveness now. Let Christ and Christ alone be glorified! Let no creature seek to share in the glory of the Creator who made them and saved them!

Human stories are messy because humans are messy. By that I mean that we are sinful and 'under construction.' As I have written this book, I have told 'His story' in my story and how I came to see that they are, in fact – wonder of wonders – 'one story.' Some names mentioned in my story were changed to protect the privacy of the person or their families. I have footnoted those names. In other cases, we have asked and received permission to mention someone's name and that person has approved that part of the story. The only caveat to this would be the matter of the oral history of my very early life given to me by my family as I grew up. Most of my family are now gone. However, my pastor, The Reverend Robert E. Baxter of Dothan, Alabama, (formerly of Olathe, Kansas, where I consider my home church to be), who also was pastor to my Aunt Eva and who witnessed much of the best side of this testimony, can vouch for the authenticity of these details.

ACKNOWLEDGEMENTS

I have written books and articles before, but I have never written a book about my life. I have found it to be a daunting undertaking, but one which frequently required me to stop writing and start praying! And in some cases, to weep with thanksgiving for our so great salvation in Jesus Christ.

I send this final draft off to a very patient publisher, with humble thanksgiving to our Savior Jesus Christ for His mercies, and to William MacKenzie for his invitation. I am also thankful to many others, such as Rebecca Rine, my editor, whose challenges made a better book, I think, and Martha Miller, my assistant, who retired as I was writing this, and April Gordon, my new assistant, who came in and so cheerfully became a ministry multiplier to me in countless ways. I thank Steve Wallace, my friend and fellow minister at First Presbyterian Church of Chattanooga. Steve and Debbie have been great blessings to us in our time here and I could not have imagined serving in this unique time in our lives without these friends. I thank the Session of First Presbyterian Church, especially our clerk of session, Scott Brown, Jr., for encouragement and prayers. I want to also thank the late Dr. D. James Kennedy, a mentor for many years, to whom I owe so much in my vocation as a believer and as a minister. He lies recovering from a very serious illness as I write, and my life feels poorer because he could not read this manuscript as he has done so graciously before. Thus, the one who helped put the story into divine perspective is now unable to share in the story's publication. To say that I am grateful for his life and ministry does not begin to tell the story of how I feel.

I save my greatest note of appreciation for my wife, Mae, and our son, John Michael, who both were great sources of encouragement as I agreed to do the work and as I sought to bring it to completion. In particular, I am thankful for Mae who read and reread the manuscript, looking at it through the singular lens of a loving wife as well as one who has joined me in the journey for twenty-two years.

John Donne once wrote:

> 'After the sermon, I will steal in to my cloak room, and pray that my good purposes may be well accepted, and my defects graciously pardoned.'

And so now I offer this, to the glory of God, and make Donne's plea my own!

Introduction

My Hope and Prayer

> 'Learning to remember well is one key to redeeming the past; and the redemption of the past is itself nestled in the broader story of God's restoring of our broken world to wholeness – a restoration that includes the past, present, and future' (Miroslav Volf, *The End of Memory).*

> 'O give thanks to the Lord, call upon his name; make known his deeds among the peoples!' (1 Chron. 16:8).

This book is not an autobiography in the same way as, say, the memoirs of an aging evangelist might be. Neither is this the book of a would-be celebrity sharing it all. No, it is not an autobiography in that sense. It is, however, a testimony of God's grace by one sinner saved by Jesus Christ and transformed to become a new human being. It is a testimony seeking a hearing. But there's more.

When the publisher approached me to write this book, I asked, 'Why me?' Mr. MacKenzie of Christian Focus gave me his answer: 'You can be a source of encouragement to others by sharing what God has done in your life. I have talked to others who have been touched by your story.'

I prayed about it, and I believed that Christ could be honored with this book and human beings could be touched by His grace. I felt that I could only write such a book if I could write it as a series of experiences granted to me by God in which I saw His comforting sovereign grace at work in a way that I could share with others. I am a pastor, and if I accepted this kind and generous offer, I wanted to speak to others in the same way that I would speak to you if you were in my study.

So, this is my aim: to share with you how God has shown me that the very things that have sought to destroy me have become, in the hands of a good God, the very things that led me to Him. What has happened to me has happened that God might show you how He will take up the broken pieces of your life and reshape them into something good, something lovely, something fitting to praise of His glorious name.

So I told Mr. MacKenzie yes.

'Change me, oh God,
Into a tree in Autumn.
And let my dying
Be a blaze of glory!'

(Esther Popel, 'October Prayer')

Thus, I write to you that you may know the love of God in Jesus Christ which is available to you, whatever your situation, whatever your pain, whatever your need.

That I may write with all the more intentionality, and that I may fulfill my own heart's desire for my family, you will notice that I have written this book in a voice that speaks directly to my son or daughter or wife – or you! I want to reach you personally with this message of God's grace in my life that you, too, may know Him. This work has been an act of remembering, and in remembering giving thanks to God. It is my prayer that it will awaken your soul to the reality of the risen Jesus Christ in your life.

This is my hope and prayer:

Lord, I pray for the one who is reading this right now. I ask, Lord, that you lead them further into this book so that seeing how you led me, this man or this woman or this child will be astonished at Your grace and moved by Your invitation to come to Jesus, and that they would come. O Lord, let them come to you with their painful past, and leave their burdens at Calvary's cross, where You bled and died for them. And let them, in some way through this testimony of mine, begin to see the empty tomb of hope for their own lives. I pray this because you have many who are not yet in the safety of the Ark of our salvation. And the waters are already beginning to come. The deluge of God's wrath against sin is already at hand. Help me, now, O Christ, to be faithful as I write, giving you all the glory, and shaping each word to the goal of presenting You to others through Your life in mine. I pray with great anticipation for blessings to come from this testimony of one sinner saved by grace and called to preach the Gospel he once shunned. In Your Name, O Jesus Christ, I pray! Amen!

1

All Blessings are Mine

> 'When thou art absent all sorrows are here.
> When thou art present all blessings are mine.'
> ('Victory,' from *The Valley of Vision)*

> 'I will restore to you the years that the swarming locust has eaten, the hopper, the destroyer, and the cutter, my great army, which I sent among you' (Joel 2:25).

I was supposed to have been aborted. But that is not my identity. I was abandoned, abused, and kidnapped – all before I was five years old. But that is not my identity. I hear folks talk about their identity in terms of their heredity – I am from English stock or I am a Choctaw Indian. I am both of those things, but that is not my identity. Some say, 'I was adopted' or 'I was orphaned' or 'My father was a drunk and my mother insane,' and that is their identity. I could, myself, use those phrases to describe my life. But that is not my identity. 'I was divorced' and 'I lost my kids' and 'I made some terrible choices' are all monikers that some use to describe their essential personhood. But not me, even though I could utter those hard confessions to you now. 'I am a successful businessman, a "golden-haired fast tracker," grooming for the vice-presidency of a major corporation. That is who I am.' I was that, too. But that is not who I am. Perhaps some in my position today would even claim, 'I am the pastor of one of the greatest churches in America.' I am a pastor, and I do think the historic First Presbyterian Church of Chattanooga, Tennessee, is a one-of-a-kind church in our nation. Being a minister and being at that particular church is an extension of my identity. But that is not who I am.

My identity is, quite simply, completely related to Jesus Christ. Some reading this will not like my saying that. They will want more. They will want 'depth.' They will want 'irony.' But He is all there is to me. I am as deep as this: I have only Him. There is no mystery, irony, or feature about me that is amazing or even interesting but that He chose me and I am His. That is the story of stories as far as I can tell. You need to know that I am not a religious man, as one might think of that term, even though I am an ordained Presbyterian minister. I am simply a disciple, a follower of Jesus of Nazareth. Sometimes I follow Him closely and sometimes I don't, to my own hurt and my own shame. But I am His. And He is mine – in the sense that He has given His life to me. I am not seeking to be super-spiritual with you. I am saying that I knew a Mike Milton before this resurrected God-Man came and revealed the Good News to me. That Mike Milton was reared with kind, aging, nurturing hands placed on his head every day of his life – as if to convey blessing (and it did) – by his Aunt Eva. That Mike Milton was baptized as an infant at Felicity Methodist Episcopal Church in the garden district of New Orleans one Sunday morning when his alcoholic father woke up from a drunken stupor, remembered his childhood of faith, put on a clean shirt, took his baby boy out of the mess he had brought him into, and sought to make peace with God – and somehow trust in a God of grace that would make something good out of the boy's life. That Mike Milton –

orphaned and placed by the courts into the custody of his father's sister, Eva Turner, a sixty-five-year-old widow who lived on a little piece of ground with some chickens in a rural, poverty-stricken area north and east of Baton Rouge going up toward Amite County, Mississippi – did not know God. He would walk an aisle in a Baptist church at age seven, get immersed, all wet in covenant waters, again. But his mind was not wet, his soul was not saturated with Christ alone. It was an immersion of the body but not the soul. That Mike Milton, who could never remember a time when he didn't hear the name of Jesus, could not understand the words of the Puritan:

> 'I bless thee for the happy moment when I first saw thy law fulfilled in Christ, wrath appeased, death destroyed, sin forgiven, my soul saved.'

The Mike Milton I am speaking of was not saved. I really mean that. He was a lost soul. You know what I mean because someone reading this feels that way about herself. This fellow was a sinner who knew the Bible, a sinner who eventually even knew how to preach and who was a lay preacher. He was so far from home, so far away from the God of his dear Aunt Eva, and nothing he did could get him back. But that lost soul, that Mike Milton, that poor boy, is gone. He was destroyed by sin and shame. He was born once and lived out the life of a soul that was infected and diseased. I am not saying that God healed the disease. I am saying that there had to be a transplant. I am saying that the man who writes these words is a new man. I was born again. I don't mean to throw religious words at you, friend. It is just that the words of Jesus in John 3 literally describe exactly what happened in my own life. I was one man before and another man after He met me and called me. I knew of Him, but until my heart was opened to His sovereign presence and power and until I knew that I was justified before God by His death, covered in His righteousness, I was a religious person who was lost. Once I was born again, I began a life as a disciple of the Christ of the Scriptures, by His grace alone and through faith alone. According to my Master, the Carpenter from Nazareth whom I now love, that life is an eternal life. That eternal life has already started. I am subject to sin and shame in this world and in this flesh, but by His grace, I am moving closer to Him, closer to a day when He will complete in me what He has started.

I am writing to tell you what happened to me. I am writing to testify to the resurrected and living Lord of life, our Savior Jesus Christ. I am writing because He is my life and I want Him to be yours. You might say, 'Why do you want that for me? You don't even know me.' All right then, let's say that I am writing to my son. If I am writing to my son, and in a real way I am, I want to say, 'I want Him to be yours.' I want that because this Lord and Savior has called me, as He does each and every one who follows him, to go and make disciples, and love compels us to do so. His Spirit, living in us, guiding us, teaching us, and comforting us, grants great pleasure in teaching others whatever He has said. He is the Living Water, and you may be thirsty. He is the Living Bread come down from heaven, and you may be hungry. He is life, and you may be dying. Why wouldn't I want you to have Him? This is why I write.

But I want to know this: What is your identity?

As I write, I am in Washington, D.C., to present a paper to the Evangelical Theological Society. Tonight I took a walk and sought out a restaurant where I could enjoy supper. Near Dupont Circle I saw a Thai place. For some reason Thai sounded very good to me, so I went in. As I walked in, I could tell that the young, hip clientele of Dupont Circle, the staffers and the aides to the Washington power-brokers, frequented this restaurant. The place was, as they say, hopping. A big, oversized plasma television mounted on the wall behind the brassy bar pulsated high definition pictures of all the world had to offer – entertainment, glamour, sex, power. Speakers were blaring, not the television audio, but a cut from a rock song I remembered from my own adolescence. It is now considered 'retro.' Images and sound, discordant but unified in their empty but attractive message, provided a backdrop – a sort of soundtrack and video – for the lives of those gathered there that night. As I was being seated by the Thai server, we passed the young patrons at the bar – a young twenty-ish man with a cigarette in one hand and an amber-colored drink on the rocks in the other, leaning into a willowy blond, obviously trying to impress her. I remembered. I remembered when I saw the young career men meeting, planning, and giving it all to get ready for what appeared to be a big meeting with a big man tomorrow morning. I remembered. I listened – I had no choice actually – to the rather shrill voice of a thirty-something, tweedy sort of fellow next to me trying to impress a girl with his knowledge of jazz. She just seemed to look down as he talked, twirling her Thai noodles without ever eating them. I remembered. I remembered what life was like when I was searching for an identity through relationships and big plans and big dreams and wild schemes. I remembered. They all seemed so sad as they laughed and smoked and flirted. It is all very human and very normal. I do not distance myself from it as if I am better. I know the truth; I am not. It is just that I have been found. I am out of the rat race of ambition and of trying to prove myself. I didn't get out of it because I was smart enough or strong enough or witty enough. I got out because the whole thing blew up. My life – starting as it did, with sorrow, then hope, then sorrow, then utter despair – just stopped. And out of the explosion of my own destruction, I was born again. I began to live. I began to breathe. I felt what a smoker feels like after he quits smoking and says, 'I never knew that strawberry ice cream tasted like this! I never knew that the air actually had a sweet smell in the early morning of summer. I can taste! I can breath! I can smell!' That is the way I felt when Jesus came into my life. The old Mike died. A new man was born. It was all – I am telling you, ALL – because of the love and grace of this Man of Galilee. I love Him, and through His love and power, the things that have sought to destroy me are not my identity. He is. The Lord Jesus Christ is my identity. I have learned

> 'When thou art absent all sorrows are here.
> When thou art present all blessings are mine.'

Let me tell you – and yes, I TRULY AM talking to you, son; to you, honey; to you, my love; to you, my flock; to you, my students; as well as to you, dear madam or sir whom I shall never meet – let me tell you about how this came to be, because if God did this with me….

2

Thou Hast Made Me

> 'Thou hast made me and shall Thy work decaye?' (John Donne).
>
> 'Before I formed you in the womb I knew you, and before you were born I consecrated you; I appointed you a prophet to the nations' (Jer. 1:5).

My identity as a son of God through Jesus Christ is the essential attribute of my life today. I am the son of the living God who adopted me into His family. Nothing gives me more strength than the doctrine of adoption. I love being adopted. It means I was chosen out of love. My Aunt Eva, who reared me and who adopted me, used to tell me that. Being adopted means I am special. I was chosen out of love. I keep saying that over and over again because it has transformed my life. 'God so loved the world that He gave His only begotten Son…'

DNA does not make a father or a mother. Love does. Not just any love, but a parent's love forged by God Himself. Covenantal commitment to be a mother or a father is more powerful and more influential than biology, so God's love, shown to me in Aunt Eva's love, is my legacy. But I am way, way ahead of myself. Let me start again, for coming to this understanding of my identity in Jesus Christ was a tremendous epiphany that changed my life for the better. Or rather, gave me a new and better life.

My life began through an ill-fated meeting of two alcoholics in a treatment center in New Orleans. At least that is what I was told. It is certain that the couple had nothing in common other than their pain.

Jessie Ellis Milton was one of eight children of George Michael and Louise Milton of Walker, Louisiana, a rural community in Southeastern Louisiana (it used to be called Milton Old Fields, having been named after the pioneer of that area, an Englishman by the name of Michael Milton, one of four brothers who made their way from Virginia, having hailed from parts unknown in Great Britain). They were Methodists – of the Calvinistic kind (then were they from Wales, where such Methodism flourished under the preaching of Whitefield?) – and strong believers in Christ. They were not poor in the sense of being hungry and homeless on the street. They had little, but what they had, they worked for. They were industrious, civic minded, and patriotic. They were farmers, and farmers of that hardy variety that one may still see in parts of England and Wales and Scotland today. When I have traveled to the old country, I have seen their warm, rounded faces with large blue eyes looking out from visible eyelids. My family was not of the southern aristocratic kind, so the War Between the States was just 'the Civil War' in my growing-up memories. They had not owned slaves, had not owned a plantation, and did not care to be fighting a 'rich man's war.' My great-grandfather served with a regiment out of Louisiana but left during the war to come home and tend to the farm. He lost nothing either before or after the war. The family of my father was not like some I know, where being southern was an honor. I never heard any of that. We were just Americans. That's all.

But the farming life was not the life that my father wanted. Jessie Ellis Milton had always wanted to see the world. His boyhood dreams of leaving the piney woods and the plowed earth of Livingston Parish to see the great ports of Britain and Europe and Africa and Asia became reality for him at a young age. He went into the Merchant Marine as a sixteen-year-old boy. This was about the year 1928. By the time Japan attacked Pearl Harbor, Jessie Ellis Milton had gone through officers' school in New London, Connecticut. He was now serving, as the Merchant Marine did, under the Department of the Navy. During World War II he commanded a ship carrying troops and supplies from New York to Liverpool. There was another part of his life, however. Ellis Milton was married to a woman named Annie Mae. I wish I could have known her.[1] She was a schoolteacher. Kindhearted, warm, and very devoted to Ellis, she nevertheless was alone, and she pleaded for him to come home. He did for a while. He tried various jobs, even keeping an inn at one time, but it failed because he was failing. Like so many men on the sea, he succumbed to the sins of womanizing and alcohol. While trying to recover a damaged marriage to a good woman, Ellis Milton left it all and returned to his mistress, the sea. Free, then, from a wife – they divorced – Ellis Milton sailed far, far away. He went even further away from the God he knew as a child when he was safe in the bosom of a godly community where Jesus Christ was preached and the family was taught, sometimes by a Methodist circuit rider who ministered to this farming family. So a godly upbringing, a naval education, and honorable service to his country were eclipsed by the demons of alcoholism.

This is how he got to New Orleans to be treated for his alcoholism. And this is how he met 'Marina'[2]. Marina was

---

[1] God tied up many loose ends in my life, but I never did get to meet this woman named Annie Mae who was my father's wife. My aunt knew her, sometimes saw her, and she never remarried. She died, I was told, in the early 1990s, having lived all of those years in Louisiana as a 'Mrs. Milton.'

[2] This is not her name. Out of respect for her family, I do not wish to reveal her identity.

a half-breed Choctaw Indian from Mississippi. I know nothing of her parentage. She, too, had already been married and divorced at least twice, I think, and was also an alcoholic, as I have said. That she suffered from schizophrenia and other diseases of the mind as a result of her alcoholism, I am certain. I mention that because of my next statement. My aunt told me that after my conception, Marina felt the best thing to do was to have an abortion. Abortions were not as common then as they are now. In our world, where more than one million abortions happen every year, this desire might not shock our sensibilities perhaps like it would have then. Ellis Milton pleaded for the child. He would raise it. So, out of drunkenness, loneliness, disobedience, mental illness, and sin, and despite attempts to snuff out my life before I could breathe my first breath, on February 26, 1958, the child of this mismatched, alcoholic couple was born at the Touro Infirmary in New Orleans, Louisiana. Later in my life I lived out some February days in New Orleans. February days in New Orleans can be bitter cold, with the dampness that chills to the bone coming off the Mississippi River. It is not like the snowy weather in the Midwest or in Tennessee where I live now. I used to call it 'pneumonia weather' because that is what it would give you if you stayed out in it. I can only imagine that day, covered, as it must have been, under the Spanish moss of the Live Oaks that line St. Charles Avenue, where sunlight fights to filter through the trees. On that day, when confusion and shame covered what should have been a happy moment in life, joy struggled to filter in through the overgrowth of sin.

Were they married or not? I do not know, but they began to live together after I was born. I have seen the house on St. Charles Avenue where we lived. My father, the naval officer, was now a repairman in a hotel when he was not out to sea on a Merchant Marine vessel. It was in that house, on the three-hundred block of St. Charles, I was told by my aunt, that my mother – and she must have been drinking heavily – tied me up and placed me in a doghouse. I was told that my father found me there with police in tow. The arrangement between the two was over. It would be attempted again later but never for more than a few days when Marina would come to see me. The attempt at a 'normal' family had failed. Alcoholism and its attendant manias had robbed all hope from the couple.

I guess if you were hoping to write a script for the life of a man who would one day be a minister, this wouldn't be it. But let me ask you this: Can God work through your weaknesses, your trials, and your peculiar heartaches?

As I write, I am reading a Puritan named Thomas Watson. He wrote,

> 'To know that nothing hurts the godly, is a matter of comfort; but to be assured that all things which fall out shall co-operate for their good, that their crosses shall be turned into blessings, that showers of affliction water the withering root of their grace and make it flourish more; this may fill their hearts with joy till they run over.'

Sometimes I hear of a writer, usually a celebrity, who, trying to pen their life's story, comes to the pain of their past. They speak of that moment as if that was the defining moment of their lives, as if they became victims of some pain – a rape, a beating, or the loss of a loved one – which they can never run away from.

Well, here is the thing that I am experiencing even as I write about this: I am praising God. I say again, I am not trying to be a super saint here. It is just that as I look at this cross, I can see how God turned it to a blessing. I observe these showers of affliction that came upon me early on by being born into such shame and misery, and I say with the old Puritan that this has watered the withering root of grace and made it flourish more.

My father must have picked me up, cleaned me up, and thought about what he should do. I was told that Marina was committed to a mental health care hospital. I would not really know her for some time. She would come in and out of my life until I was about four years of age. But what my father did next became one of the most important things – and maybe the most important thing – that has ever happened to me. My father must have walked down St. Charles Avenue to one of those old grocery stores that seem to be all over New Orleans and borrowed a telephone. He called for my aunt who lived in Baton Rouge – Aunt Georgia – and her kind-hearted husband, a godly businessman from Tennessee – Uncle John Taylor – who often ministered to my ailing father, giving him money and helping him when he was down. Aunt Georgia and Uncle John went to help Ellis, her older brother, once more. Everyone had wondered how long it would take for this day to come – the day when Ellis and Marina would call it quits, the day when Ellis could no longer care for his little son born out of such shame. I can guarantee that Aunt Georgia and Uncle John didn't calculate those things. She has told me herself that they got into the car and immediately began the journey down Airline Highway, across the bayous and swamps, to the old section of New Orleans where my father and I waited. They came to get me, and Ellis told them, 'Bring him to Eva.'

3

An Angel Named Aunt Eva and the Sawdust of Heaven

'If thy mercy make me poor and vile, blessed be thou! Prayers arising from my needs are preparations for future mercies' (From the prayer, 'The Divine Will' in *The Valley of Vision*).

'To her God was all in all, and her access to God she found only through the new and living way that the Scriptures point out. I do not see how anyone could know my mother well without being forever sure that whatever else there may be in Christianity, the real heart of Christianity is found in the atoning death of Christ' (J. Gresham Machen).

'For this child I prayed, and the Lord has granted me my petition that I made to him. Therefore I have lent him to the Lord. As long as he lives, he is lent to the Lord' (1 Sam. 1:27-28).

Eva Milton Turner was my father's sister. When I was nine months old, she became my mother. She had never had children of her own, having married a man much older than she. Though he had grown children, close to her age, they never came to visit and she spoke little of them. Perhaps this was because her husband, John Turner, a storekeeper and farmer who had immigrated to Louisiana from North Carolina, had just died. Aunt Eva was a widow recovering from a funeral on one day, and the next day, she was given a child.

My life's story changed at that moment.

I cannot begin to tell you the impact that Aunt Eva has had on my life. I miss her so, even now as I write. As I was growing up, there was never a day in my life when she did not pray for me, read the Bible to me, and speak to me about God's plan for my life. I have known many wise people, but I have never known anyone as wise as Aunt Eva. Some have called her an angel. If an angel is a messenger from God to do God's bidding on this earth and to speak to God's people about His will for our lives, then she was an angel. She was, at least, an angel to me.

Aunt Eva told me that on that day when she received me, she committed me to the work of the Lord, and she began a ministry, on that little 'hardtack' farm, of rearing me unto the Lord. However, during those years between my first and my sixth birthday, her work was often interrupted. It was interrupted by abuse.

Marina came and went out of our lives. The courts, recognizing the obvious mental problems that Marina had and the work responsibilities that my father had on the sea, agreed with my father's decision for me to be in the legal custody of Aunt Eva. But that didn't stop Marina from trying to see me. When she came, she would take me to a house that was a house of horrors for me. The small house, partially finished, was actually my father's house that he had built across the field from Aunt Eva (and, by this time, across from my grandmother's place, also built to keep her near Aunt Eva so she could care for her in her older years). Marina would take me to my father's house, whether he was there or not. I can remember so many things from those years, but I remember little of that house except the beatings. Marina, I am sure, was responding to something that I did (at two or three or four years of age) when she would beat me with a belt. But can a four-year-old child – can any human being – ever do anything to deserve such violence?

She would beat me with the buckle end of the belt. I can recall, quite plainly, a particular time – I have been told that I was four years old – seeking to crawl out of range of the oncoming buckle. I crawled out onto the porch. It was summer because I remember the South Louisiana heat rushing over me like a firestorm as I rolled on the linoleum floor across the threshold to the grey-painted planks of the front porch. My skin was stinging from the strap, my bones hurting from the buckle, and I shook with fear. But she pursued me with that belt. I went into a ball, a fetal position, on that front porch, and I will never forget as long as I live the image of Marina rearing back, like a baseball pitcher, and coming down, belt buckle first, onto my arms which covered my face. Perhaps she was drunk, I don't remember. But my Aunt Eva and my grandmother – quite elderly – heard me screaming and both came running across the little field that separated us, and they physically intervened.

The scene was violent, and the scene of adult women fighting was as frightening to me as the belt buckle. How does a child of four years of age know what a curse word is? But I knew. Marina hurled evil words – yes, I intuitively knew they were evil – at my Aunt Eva and my grandmother. I never heard an evil word against anyone ever come from my Aunt Eva's lips in all of her ninety-eight years, so I am certain that her response was simply to get me out as quickly as she could. The rescue was complete, and the safest place in the world for this little fellow was her lap. It would be that way, for it was in Aunt Eva's lap that I heard the Bible, received her prayers and her 'Hannah-like' blessings. I wanted to call her 'Mama.' I did try, but Aunt Eva, sensing the pain it might cause Marina, wouldn't allow it. As a result, I have never called any woman 'mother' in my life until I married my Mae. Out of teaching our son to call her 'Mom' I, like so many other husbands, called and still call her 'Mom.' But as a child? Never.

Awful scenes like I just described were not common during these days, but they happened. On another time after that, Marina came and my father was home. Aunt Eva, dutifully, took me over. I know she must have hated doing it. The two of them – Aunt Eva and Marina – obviously did not get along. This time, however, Marina asked me if I would like some ice cream. My father must have sensed that something was up, but I don't remember him protesting. It was not like there was an ice cream stand in the neighborhood! We lived way back in the country. We would have to drive into Watson to go to the Red and White Food store to get ice cream, but I guess that is what she had planned. We got into this old black Ford with torn seat covers and a bad smell (likely the stale stink of the filterless Camels she smoked), and she drove off. We drove and we drove and we drove. We drove until night. There was no ice cream, but I didn't ask any questions! She had kidnapped me. I am not sure where we went, but I am almost certain, now, it must have been to her relatives in Mississippi. I remember an old man and an old woman, wrinkled, toothless, tanned if not dark-skinned by nature, smiling but not touching. I was frightened of them. I remember seeing the earth, wet and mossy with heat and humidity, through the planks of their cabin-like floor. We stayed there for – I have no idea how long – and then she returned. My aunt and father and grandmother and a Livingston Parish sheriff's deputy were waiting as we returned. I have no idea today how, at that moment, I got from the car to Aunt Eva's arms, but I know this: I never saw Marina again until I was an adult.

It would be good to say that, at that moment, all of the problems ended for me. But my father, increasingly troubled by his alcoholism, lost his job (I was told later as I grew up) and spent more time at home. That meant that I would go and spend time with him. What do I remember?

I remember the smell of alcohol. I remember my father plopped down in an oversize chair, drinking whiskey out of the bottle and smoking his Camels. I remember that in Aunt Eva's house was a nicely framed photograph of this man as a young Naval lieutenant. He was handsome and clean and smiling in his smart and honorable dress uniform. I remember looking at my father and noticing the contrast. He was drunk, crying, and alternating between a whiskey bottle and a guitar or violin (he played both and played well). He was dressed, not in a uniform or a suit, but in trousers and an undershirt that was too big for him, making him appear all the more weak and puny and sick. He cursed and, as I said, he cried. Seeing my father in this condition made me sad and even confused. 'Why would he do this to himself?'

One time I thought I would help him. After he fell into a drunken sleep, I had an idea. I must have been around five years old, about a year before he died. I crept into the kitchen where I found a bottle. I reached up on the counter, grabbed the bottle and headed to the bathroom. I dumped the contents into the drain. The liquor gurgled as it filled up the sink and then disappeared, slowly, into the drain. The whole house smelled of whiskey! I then filled the whiskey bottle with tap water. What a devious little fellow I was! And how innocent was my plan: he will think he is drinking that stuff, but he will just be drinking water! He will then not get sad or cry or get drunk. It never occurred to me that there could be some difference between the taste of water and the taste of whiskey. After I carried out my bit of espionage, I ran outside, fearful and yet triumphant. 'Mission accomplished' was the feeling I had. Aunt Eva and my grandmother were outside. I ran to them and told them what happened. I remember that they laughed together, grabbed me, and we all embraced as if the plan would, in fact, work and we would all be free of the 'demons.' But the sleeping alcoholic, my father, awoke. He found out what I did. He was still drunk, and he got very angry, though

I can never remember my father angry any other time. He whipped me. I wept not only from the beating, but also from the failure of my father to see that I was trying to help him. I remember asking Aunt Eva – I was four years old – 'When will this nightmare end?' I had heard that spoken somewhere, and it seemed like the right question. But four-year-olds should not be looking at life as a nightmare. They should not have to wonder when it would go away. It just shouldn't be there.

Let me pause here. Some of you reading this are the children or spouses of alcoholics. I pray for you now. May the hope of Jesus Christ, who is the Redeemer of our souls and our bodies and our families and our emotions and our everything, bring you peace. May those of you under the powerful sway of addiction be given the power of faith in Jesus Christ that your chains may be broken! Your family will run to you in joy. Your husband or wife, your little ones, your adult children – they will all bless the God of Israel who snapped the chains of your bondage. I am no psychiatrist, no mental health expert. I am only the son of an alcoholic, I am only a pastor, but I have seen God work. With Him nothing is impossible! Oh, that you may have hope in God!

My Aunt Eva taught me that. She believed that God could heal my father. She believed that God used the prayers of the Church to work miracles in our world today. My Aunt Eva had been reared in a Calvinistic Methodist home, as I said. Yet, she had married a Baptist from North Carolina. She submitted to immersion and joined the Baptist church, but after her husband died and by the time I came along, she went wherever she could get a ride. You see, Aunt Eva had never driven a car in her life. It is not that she didn't drive because she didn't have a car. It is that she had no idea how to drive one of those things! She was always dependent upon a ride from someone else.

There were three kinds of places for a person to go to church in our little rural community: the Baptist church, the Methodist church, and several independent movements that had broken away from one or the other. We could get a ride to the Baptist church, so that is where we went (My grandmother would not go. She said, 'I was born a Methodist and I will die a Methodist!' and she did; but her minister, a faithful man of God, brought Communion to her regularly until she died. I will never forget that kind minister, and I hope that I, too, can be used of God to show His love to others in that way). However, one of those independent works sprang up alongside the unpaved road that led to our home. Aunt Eva thought that if the Word of God was being preached and we were that close, we ought to go and support the preaching of the Word. This was a little rough-hewn, pinewood chapel, and it had sawdust on the floor. They called it 'the Tabernacle.'

The Tabernacle seated about thirty people if those people were all crowded together and some stood in the back! We would walk down there on Wednesday evenings. I remember so well walking down the lane, holding Aunt Eva's hand, and hearing the singing that was 'warming up' in that place. To be honest, I was a bit fearful of that place as a young lad. They sang louder than the Baptists, and they used instruments like tambourines, banjos, guitars, and the accordion – their instrument of choice (they didn't have enough money to buy a piano or an organ). Some of the people there were Pentecostal, of the devout holiness groups, and others were probably just 'dissenters' from the 'established' churches. The women who attended the Tabernacle wore their hair high and lifted up! They wore long skirts, all the way to the floor, and so did their daughters. They looked different from the women I had seen, whether Aunt Eva or other women at the Baptist and Methodist churches. The men wore denim overalls to church. This was very different from the Methodists and the Baptists (unless it was 'old timey day' when the men might wear overalls, but that was more of a spoof!). But Aunt Eva said we were there 'not for the show' – and that is the way she put it, to be honest with you – but we were there to 'hear the Word of God' and to 'pray with the saints.'

The Word of God was delivered by a preacher with the name of 'Brother Devall.' He was a Frenchman who drove there from another part of the Parish. He was not from our community. Though Louisiana is known for the Cajuns today, there were none where I was reared – only English and Scotch-Irish farming stock. One thing is for certain: Brother Devall, a plumber by day and preacher by night, could pray. I cannot remember how he preached (whereas I can remember the preaching of the Baptists and the Methodists very well). But he seemed to be a gentle man, and I wasn't afraid of him at all (which is, as I look back at it, a very good indication that he was a pastoral sort of fellow).

Those services were really prayer meetings. Even today I cannot hear the word 'prayer meeting' without thinking of the Tabernacle's prayer meetings. That prayer meeting, I learned, is what caught the interest of Aunt Eva. She wanted her brother, my father, to repent and return to Almighty God. She believed that only God could do it and that prayer was His way of involving us in my father's life and His will. And do you know what? Those Pentecostals and Independents believed it too. I can remember hearing my father's name being lifted up in prayer in that place. They were praying that my father would be saved, saved from hell and saved from himself. They prayed as if God could and would answer their prayers. I remember that in their prayer meetings, much was made of the blood of Jesus Christ on the cross. They looked to His sacrifice as their avenue for answered prayer. I heard of and knew what 'Calvary' and 'Golgotha' meant by the time I was five years old, and I knew it because that is what the Tabernacle people prayed about all of the time. They pled the blood of Jesus before the throne of His Father for the life of my father.

After these Wednesday night prayer meetings, Aunt Eva and I would walk home together, hand-in-hand, down that little lane. It would be pitch dark (there were no street lights out in the country, of course). In the summer you could hear the locusts singing and see the stars way up in the sky. The locusts and the stars and the quiet made you feel the impression left by the praying voices and the jingle-jangle of the tambourines and the roaring of the singing in that little chapel. You could feel it all at once in your soul. We would not talk as we walked. It all seemed to a five-year-old what one might call 'magic.' But I didn't know what magic was. I knew it was God.

My father repeatedly rejected my Aunt Eva's pleas. I remember hearing her sobbing before him to 'come on up to the Tabernacle, Ellis; it will do you so much good.' I remember seeing her begging him to come. She would say, 'Come for your son, Ellis! Do it for him! Just come with us to the Tabernacle!' My father always resisted. He never outright refused. Rather, he always 'conveniently' had another plan for that evening (not that there was anything else whatsoever to do where we lived!). My father continued to go in and out of alcoholic bouts during these days. By this time, the summer before I would turn six years old (February 26th), I was living and sleeping every night at Aunt Eva's – to be truthful, sleeping with Aunt Eva! I loved sleeping next to her. All of the sorrow and heartache and pain seemed to go away during those nights.

One Wednesday evening, and I have no idea how it happened, my father accepted Aunt Eva's invitation. Aunt Eva was older than my father. She had changed his diaper when he was a baby. Aunt Eva was a sort of 'holy woman' to my father. No doubt, she finally used some power she had over him to convince him. That night, the three of us walked hand–in-hand, down the gravel lane, up to the Tabernacle. As we walked, we could hear the happy music starting. That night we took our seats on the pine benches on the next to the last pew on the congregation's left-hand side of the chapel. We stood and sang 'Amazing Grace' – accordions and tambourines and guitars and banjos playing full blast – and then, still standing, Brother Devall opened the service in a great prayer, full of God's glory, our sin, Jesus' blood atonement for sin, God's love and God's forgiveness through faith in Jesus Christ. The congregation was seated, and my father began weeping. He put his head down in his hands, and he was crying like a child. He slipped out of his seat, onto the sawdust floor. The chapel was totally quiet except for my father's sobs. He was sitting between me and Aunt Eva. She put her arm around him. Brother Devall came down from behind his piney pulpit and walked over to my father. I was sitting right there. Brother Devall spoke words to him, but I couldn't make out what he was saying. Then, one by one, the entire congregation, including the female accordion player with her high hair and her long dress, came over to my father. They laid their hands on him or on the closest person they could get to. I couldn't breathe. There were so many people, and some were crying, and I was under it all, next to my weeping father. I sensed that something huge had happened in my father's life.

My father did not drink anymore after that summer night in 1963. He also began going to church again. I remember him as smiling. He wore his suits again, with his dress hat. He seemed content. On Wednesday, April 29th, 1964, my father walked across the way to Aunt Eva's house. I was in the big porch swing on the front porch of that hundred-year-old farmhouse. I was now six years old but not yet in school. He said that he came to say goodbye to me, and he told me that he was sorry. I didn't know what he had done to say that, and I was alarmed that an adult would say such a thing to a child. Such things were not heard. I didn't know why but I felt, to be honest, annoyed by it. Or maybe confused. I don't know, and I can't remember my feelings exactly, except that I now regret not falling before him and telling him how much I loved him. He turned and walked away. I saw his tall, lanky figure move away from the porch, across Aunt Eva's yard, and over the grassy, empty space between our house and his. I started swinging again, not knowing that I would never see my father again.

The next morning, my Uncle John, ever faithful to his sick brother-in-law, drove his Buick out to our place, picked up my father in the early hours, and drove him to a hospital. Uncle John later told me that during the trip from the country to the hospital, my father gave him his wallet and told him where all of his valuables were located, not that he had much by that time. Uncle John protested and even laughed. But my father was serious. Uncle John escorted him into the hospital and saw that he got checked in, for what exactly I have never asked. The next day, May 1, 1964, the hospital called to say that my father had died unexpectedly. I was under the covers, for it was chilly that morning. The telephone rang. I could hear Aunt Eva. I could hear her say, 'Ellis? What?' And I knew my father was dead.

I shall always remember, in May, in another world so far away from the place where I am today, the rain that fell on the steel gray coffin of my father as six men – I don't know who they were – carried the remains of my daddy to his grave at Palmetto Cemetery, the old Methodist cemetery in Walker, Louisiana, which used to be called Milton Old Field.

This I know: because the Tabernacle people believed, because Aunt Eva persisted, because of the blood of Jesus Christ, and a drunkard's faith, I will see my father again. Every time I smell sawdust, I think of heaven.

4

Poor and Didn't Know it

> 'Help me to see how good thy will is in all, and when it crosses mine teach me to be pleased with it. Grant me to feel thee in fire, and food and every providence, and to see that thy many gifts and creatures are but thy hands and fingers taking hold of me.' (From 'The All Good' in *The Valley of Vision*).

> 'O God, from my youth you have taught me, and I still proclaim your wondrous deeds' (Ps. 71:17).

My son, my daughter, my grandchild, my student, my flock – dear reader – I feel compelled by the Spirit of the Lord to pause at this point. I want you to know that 'what has happened to me has really served to advance the gospel' (Phil. 1:12) and that through the prayers and teaching and ministry of my Aunt Eva 'and the help of the Spirit of Jesus Christ this [turned] out for my deliverance' (Phil. 1:19). You must not feel that I am a victim. The Lord chose me from the foundation of the earth, as He did you, if you prove that divine election by your trusting wholly in the Savior, and thus 'He also preserves me in such a way that without the will of my heavenly Father not a hair can fall from my head; indeed, all things must work together for my salvation' (as it says in that wonderfully encouraging Heidelberg Catechism question and answer one). In this chapter I want to share with you how God worked in my life, at an early age, to prepare me for Himself. This is important for you, for if you are wandering from God because of some affliction or pain that has frightened you, or you are ignoring God because you could not see His hand in the things that happened to you, or if your own dark unbelief is blinding you to His goodness, then let this reflection from my own life lift your eyes toward heaven. He is not absent in your pain. My friend, be sure of this: He is not even absent in your unbelief! For while you are still a long way off, the Father runs toward you! The Father, who desires that you not perish but have eternal life, who desires that you return to Him, the One you know exists because you sense Him and have groped, albeit in the dark, for His presence, He desires you to be His own. He prepares you for His good will even when you are a babe in the woods. That is what this chapter is all about.

I was poor but didn't know it. After Marina left the scene, after my father's alcoholism was 'cured' by Christ, and after He was called home, life settled down. It is true that my grandmother died soon after my father died, but she was elderly. I cannot remember much of her except a sort of gruffness that I had never known in a woman. Aunt Eva, you must understand, was never anything but sweet to me. She worked hard and sometimes if she hit her finger with a hammer, say while repairing the fence out in the pasture, she would not curse but would say, 'Thank you Lord!' Afterward, as she mended her wound, she would explain to me that the blow could have been worse and that pain meant that God's design for her body was working perfectly! This was the daily way that she applied the Gospel.

We had, as I have shown you, no man in the house. My Uncle John, the only male figure in our family, was a long way off in Baton Rouge. He came out for a few hours each week on Sunday afternoons, but other than that, it was just me and Aunt Eva. Our little homestead – about six acres – was the remnant of a much larger farm that Aunt Eva's deceased husband used to farm. What we had left was enough for a pretty good size chicken yard, an old barn with stables, and five acres of pastureland for several cows, a horse (my pet), and at various times sheep or goats. I also had a dog named Snooper – a pretty, good-natured mix that looked like the effect of a Corgi and Collie liaison – and a cat named Mr. Tom. Mr. Tom came in and out of our lives through my childhood, finally leaving one day to go off and die. Snooper was a devoted friend. He stayed with me through my childhood until I was sixteen years old. Our neighbor, who lived across a field, also provided Aunt Eva with enough farmland to tend several rows of crops. In this field, in this pasture, in this chicken yard, in that barn and stables, and in the woods and creeks and pastures around our place, I grew up.

Each morning included a hearty breakfast and then chores. I never remember Aunt Eva using that word. It was somehow understood that she needed me and that without me the farm could not go on. That gave me a sense of responsibility that I have carried with me through all of my life. I loved our chickens, if one can love a chicken. I will never forget the time that Aunt Eva wanted me to kill the rooster, a Rhode Island Red beauty, for our dining pleasure. I wrung his neck, but he was still alive. Aunt Eva put him on a chopping block fashioned out of an old stump, and there he lay. She handed me the ax, moved back, put her hands on her hips and waited. I looked at the poor creature, remembering the times I had watched him as he ruled the roost and impressed the many hens with his proud strutting. I recalled the many mornings that his early morning crowing had awakened me to pull back the blinds in my room and feel the fresh morning air coming into my lungs. I remembered, and so I dropped the ax and ran as fast as

I could, crying all the way. Aunt Eva never said anything to me, but I never saw that rooster again. She did the job herself.

There were many such times, many lessons, and many good memories. That is what that period of my childhood was all about. We were poor, living off those chickens, a few cows (they were there to provide spring calves), and those few rows of crops. We did pretty well together.

Aunt Eva read to me every day of my life, as I have said. She read the Bible or Bible storybooks. My view of the world, of people, of life, was shaped by the lives of the ancient people of God in Israel and the stories from the New Testament. I will always cherish the many times I was in her lap, hearing her voice tell me about Adam and Eve who lost Eden by their sin, or Enoch who walked with God, or the Tower of Babel and man's rebellion against God, or Abraham, the man who responded to God's call though he knew not where he was being called. One of my favorite stories from those days in Aunt Eva's lap was the Shunammite woman's boy who died in 2 Kings 4. In the story, Elisha the Prophet would make rounds in his preaching ministry. This kind woman from Shunam would prepare the prophet a room and take care of him. That woman reminded me of Aunt Eva. She loved to pray for and encourage pastors.

Once, the Methodist minister from our little community went through some very hard times. I found out later that his wife had left him – literally left him in the parsonage and moved out all of a sudden. It was said that she didn't like the ministry and didn't want to be married to a preacher anymore. This is the same minister who used to bring Communion to my grandmother. Aunt Eva's response was not only to pray for the pastor, with me, but to also chastise others for talking about him. 'He is a man of God and the Lord will take care of him. Besides, what sin has he committed? Pray for his wife and pray for the minister.' She invited him out to our house and cooked for him. She said that to have a minister in our home was a blessing from God. It didn't matter to her that he was a marked man, a man who was going to be moved out of that community by the Bishop because of the scandal his wife had created.

How different that is from what I see too often today. The ministry is likely responsible for lowering the esteem that the flock holds for it by dabbling in worldly vocations and methodologies that aim to build them up. These techniques, of course, do just the opposite. Elisha was held in honor because of the Word. We who are pastors and evangelists and teachers ought to minister through the 'ordinary means of grace' – Word, Sacrament and Prayer – and not succumb to the ways of the world to build up the ministry. Our people, also, ought to remember that God who calls His preacher boys will also sustain them and even chasten them when necessary. The concept of the holy is easily diminished. How I pray that God will stir our hearts again for the things of God.

Aunt Eva was the Shunammite woman, and in my mind, I was that boy. You see, in the story Elisha gives the Shunammite woman the desire of her heart for all of her kindnesses shown to him. In the story, she never asked for the child, but Gehazi the servant suggested to Elisha that this was the obvious need in her life. She was too content with God, even in her pain, to even ask for the child, but she and her old husband were blessed to be holding a baby one year after Elisha made the prophecy. That was Aunt Eva. I already had my 'birth story' and 'life story' down pat by the time I was seven years old. Aunt Eva had recited how God had miraculously brought me into the world and how, through the pain of my past, even the sins of others, God had placed me in her arms. I knew that I was the answer to her heart's greatest desire and that God did not forget her, even though she was sixty-five years old when she got her blessing. She was that woman and I was that boy, a gift from God to her.

But one day, as the biblical writer continued, the father was out in the field – and I was sure it was just like the field next to our old house – and while out there the boy cried out, 'My head! My head!' – and I was sure that I understood what was happening to him because I had felt the almost unbearable heat of the South Louisiana summer sun myself. Sometimes, when I was pulling turnips, Aunt Eva would say, 'That's enough. Let's go in. It's too hot for chickens, much less human beings, to be out in these fields!' When they brought the boy back to the house and put him on the bed, he was gone. But that faithful Shunammite woman got on a donkey and went after the prophet. She believed that God would bring her boy back to life and that the prophet was the man that God had anointed for such ministry. The prophet sent his assistant back with his staff to lay on the boy to heal him. But the woman didn't want an assistant and didn't want a stick. She wanted Elisha to come. It appears clear in the text that she would settle for nothing or no one less than Elisha. I could imagine Aunt Eva holding on to Brother Devall, the lay preacher-plumber from the Tabernacle, saying, 'I will not leave you until you come heal Mike! That old Louisiana sun finally got him!'

The truth is, this happened in a way. It was not sunstroke, but asthma. I had it in a bad way. I could hardly breathe. So on a Wednesday night, after the service was over, not during the service, Aunt Eva took me and she pleaded with Brother Devall to lay his hands on me and pray for me. Now Aunt Eva had prayed herself in our home with me in her lap. But she so respected the ministry, just like the Shunammite woman, that she felt constrained to have a man of God do this and he was the closest we had! He did pray for me, and I was healed.

Another time, I was playing in a big, old Live Oak tree that was just behind the Tabernacle. I was about seven years old, maybe eight. As I attempted to leap from one limb of that tree to another, I slipped and fell about fifteen feet. My fall was halted by a barbed wire fence. You have seen pictures of unfortunate paratroopers from the 101st

Airborne who parachuted behind enemy lines the night before D-Day and ended up stranded on church towers or in the treetops. Well, that is what I looked like, but it was not a parachute caught in the trees, it was my flesh caught in the barbed wire!

I screamed as I was dangling in the fence, crying to the God of Aunt Eva to help me. The God of the Shunammite woman heard me. The back door of the Tabernacle opened and out ran Brother Devall in his denim overalls. What he was doing at the Tabernacle in the middle of the day, rather than doing his plumbing work, I still do not know to this day. But God had placed him there just at the right time. In 2 Kings 4, Elisha went to the Shunammite woman's boy, lay his body over him, and the boy sneezed seven times – an unforgettable story for me! In my story, Brother Devall ran to me, but the story shifted just a bit for my circumstance. He ran to me and he bore my weight on his body as he carefully loosened the barbed wire from the various and many points on my body. The last scene of that story was Brother Devall carrying me in his arms, blood all over his overalls, and bringing me down the gravel lane to our old house. Aunt Eva ran out on the front porch and stood in shocked silence as she witnessed the scene. Brother Devall lay me down before her on the front porch as Aunt Eva got bandages. They prayed over me, and that was it. My wounds healed in time, but the images of the story stay with me.

I knew this story. I knew the other stories. When the Baptist preacher, Dr. Pierce, came to examine me to see if I was ready to make a profession of faith, I heard him say, 'Miss Eva, that boy knows the Bible. Is he ready? I don't know, but I think so.'

I interpreted my life through these stories. I was that boy. Aunt Eva was that Shunammite woman. But later I would learn that Elisha and Brother Devall were Jesus for me. And many times in my life, I have sought to go from limb to limb in life, slipping and falling and landing, not in the soft green grass of life, but in a barbed wire fence, stuck, bleeding, hurting, and crying. Isn't that your life, too? I have known my Savior to come to me. He carries me. One day He will carry me home to lay me before my Aunt Eva in heaven. One day He will carry me all the way home.

Those childhood years were filled with 4-H calves and baseball and football and getting lost in the woods and many other things that boys do – and I have told many of these stories to the flock under my pastoral care as I have sought to illustrate the Scriptures with my own life – but let me move on. Let me move on to the years when I was twelve and thirteen and fourteen, when the haunting began, when the seeds of self doubt grew to puncture my spirit, letting in the demonic, leading me under the power of my own dark heart into the years that have cut deep ruts in my life.

Please come with me. I want to share these things with you, that we may together know the glory of God's grace by admitting the depths of our sin nature. During this time I would learn that I was poor, that I was orphaned, that I lacked an identity, and that I lost God in my doubt. But I would look back on the chapter I have written here about Bible stories and barbed wire, Aunt Eva's prayers and Brother Duvall's faith, Snooper and turnip fields, and understand that I was rich and didn't know it.

5

The Unrequited Heart

'What we have suffered weighs us down like a heavy load we long to have lifted; like an indefatigable enemy, it assails us relentlessly. The wreckage of history – a trail of shattered beauty, defiled goodness, twisted truths, streams of tears, rivers of blood, mountains of corpses – must somehow be mended' (Miroslav Volf).

'As he passed by, he saw a man blind from birth. And his disciples asked him, "Rabbi, who sinned, this man or his parents, that he was born blind?" Jesus answered, "It was not that this man sinned, or his parents, but that the works of God might be displayed in him"' (John 9:1-3).

If the only pain I ever had in my life was getting hung up in barbed wire, I would have had no problems. But there was something going on deep inside of me – in my very soul. You must remember that my Aunt Eva could not have done more. Her life and her faith were one. There was no hypocrisy for me to rebel against. The church where we belonged was a good place to be. I cannot recall if the doctrines of grace or the old Reformed faith were ever preached, but then again, I would not have been listening. But Dr. J. K. Pierce was a wonderful preacher, and his passion for reaching that community for Jesus Christ made its way into my heart.

But there were problems. The Bible says,

> 'The heart is deceitful above all things, and desperately sick; who can understand it?' (Jer. 17:9).

Let me try, now, to tell you what happened, because you may be seeing this in someone you love. I want you to know how to pray. Maybe, dear reader, you will recognize this in yourself.

There came a time in my young life where the seeds of pain planted by the world, the flesh, and the devil began to sprout. Those poison seedlings grew, and weeds grew. Sin, unchecked and unanswered by Gospel truth, began sending toxins into every area of my life. Potential, hopes, dreams, decisions, and behavior: all were affected by the toxins of sin. In short, ideas have consequences, and the ideas that were ruling in my life were not of God.

So it is in the lives of so many who cannot come to terms with the pain of their past. Anger or morbidity or depression or hatred or self-loathing or self-absorption begins to consume these people. These are people who were abused or abandoned or mistreated or violated or victimized by seeming 'chance' circumstances. The culprit, they have surmised, is their parents or their grandparents or their culture or themselves or God. They are locked down by the pain, unable to be free. They are frozen in time, unable to find their future. They are without hope. They are sinking below the line of despair. All of this starts in the soul. I know this because it started in my own soul. Oh that I could have turned then to Jesus and received His promises and surrendered my pain to Him! Oh what mourning I would have avoided.

There were several things in my past that I could not find answers to.

One was why God had allowed me to be born into the shameful situation that I was born into. Rather than thank God that this pain actually delivered me into the arms of Aunt Eva who entrusted me to Jesus, I let the question fester, like an unattended sore. Another question had to do with why God had allowed my father to die. I missed not having a father. I always kept his picture in my room. I knew from an early time in my life that I would go into the military in some way because I saw his picture every day – the picture of my father as a young Naval officer. It is hard when a boy doesn't have a father or a father figure. But let me show you a beautiful picture: it is the picture of a seventy-five-year-old woman in the back yard trying to throw a football with that fatherless boy. Let me show you a picture: it is that woman telling him, 'We don't have a man in the house, but we have the Lord, and He will take care of us.' How I regret the years I missed of not giving God glory and praise for how He ministered to me through Aunt Eva.

My life in school began to change. I moved from being the top of the class in grades, the top of the school in athletics, and the top of the class in my relationships with others, to the bottom. I had been most valuable player in baseball and football, and I had raised a state champion calf – Little Joe, a stock breed calf. I was gifted in art, speech, and writing. I say these things not to boast, for we should let others boast and not we ourselves, but in order to show you how far I fell. I fell not only from what I was but also from what I could have been.

It was during this time that I also began to learn to play guitar. I was listening, in my young adolescence, to Neil Young, Jackson Brown, Bob Dylan, and underground folk-rock groups like Mason Profit. I took my questions and my pain, not to the God of Aunt Eva, not to the God of my life, but to the existentialist, Hindu-influenced lyrics of the 1960s music movement. I practiced guitar and began to write music, influenced by these new thoughts, and began to drift further and further away from God.

My beloved brother and sister, ideas are not neutral. Be careful what goes into your heart. I know you will not get through this life without some pain. Because of the fall of man, because of the presence of sin, every area of life is infected by this cosmic rebellion against the Almighty. Thus, you will, in some area of life, be affected, you will be hurt. I am telling you from my life as well as from the truth of God's Word, don't take your pain to just anyone. Neil Young was not equipped to address my pain. He reflected, in many ways – from his screaming guitar, pensive, whining voice, and dark, foreboding words – what I was feeling. But he could not give me any answers to why I was born into such a mess or why my Daddy died or who I was and where I was going. My beloved, nothing has changed. Only God can fill the void in your life. I would later write a song to deal with this matter. I called it, 'When Only the Word Will Do.' Only God's Word can provide answers to the great questions of your life. Only the story of Jesus Christ can make sense of your own story.

If only I had heard and understood what the Slavic-American theologian, Miroslav Volf, meant when he wrote, 'That the past must and will be redeemed is a conviction essential to the Christian notion of redemption.'[1]

---

[1] Miroslav Volf, *The End of Memory: Remembering Rightly in a Violent World* (Grand Rapids, MI: Wm. B. Eerdmans Publishing Co., 2006), 42.

6

The Sins of the Fathers

> 'Thou doest not play in convincing me of sin, Satan did not play in tempting me to it, I do not play when I sink into deep mire, for sin is no game, no toy, no bauble…' (From 'Humiliation,' *The Valley of Vision*).
>
> 'Do not hold against us the sins of the fathers; may your mercy come quickly to meet us, for we are in desperate need' (Ps. 79:8 NIV).

I was seeking to push life along at sixteen years of age. I had completed almost all of my high school credit hour assignments through summer school. In fact, I was in a graduating class in my eleventh year of school rather than the customary American twelve grades. And I had options. 4-H and football and good grades (without much study or effort or interest for that matter) had presented me with several doors from which to choose. I had been urged by my guidance counselor to begin the nomination process for the Naval Academy. He talked to me and thought I had a shot. In the meantime, a school of art in the Midwest offered me a scholarship to study art. Kansas State

University was recruiting me to attend their school to study agriculture. I had many options. But I told my counselor that I wanted none of them. I wanted to go to Europe to study art from a master. I wanted to study drawing and give myself entirely to that work. Secretly, I also wanted to pursue songwriting as well. I have just mentioned five possible roads that I could have taken. In fact, I took none of them, and I chose very unwisely.

I was a disobedient young man. My Aunt likely figured out much of what I was doing. I have learned that you really can't fool your parents in these things. I was smoking, trying alcohol, and doing other things that brought shame on her good name and the name she had tried to build in me. I never used illicit drugs, was never arrested, was never involved in anything criminal. But I did 'everything' else you could think of. In fact, if it ever gets back to you that there was something I reportedly did that was immoral or dishonorable – believe it. It is probably true. My football coach warned me that I was headed down the wrong path. His words scared me but did not stop me. I was on my way to the far country. I was ready to 'spend my inheritance' no matter what. And no one was going to stop me.

That leads me to insert this thought: Often our prodigal journeys, our illicit behaviors, our 'sin binges,' are self-medicating exercises to keep the pain of the past at bay. My decisions were certainly a case in point. Don't misunderstand me: I have no one to blame but myself. My Aunt was so faithful. In light of what I had gone through as a child, no one – no one – could have done more to minister to me and bring Christ to me. But I was literally 'hell bent' on ignoring her wisdom, all so I could forget the questions of my wounded, wayward heart and maybe find some relief from the pain that would not let me go. Such are the things we do, the extremes we will go to, in order to find meaning and purpose.

So what happened? Too much to say here, and too much that is so embarrassing and hurtful that it would be foolish to repeat it. There is a biblical pattern – those whom God uses much, He crushes most. Abraham and the loss of Ishmael through his sin; Moses in the 'back forty acres' of the Midian desert because of his sin; David having to watch his children fall into sin and finally his son, Absalom, rise against him because of David's sin; Peter, despairing of hope though Christ was raised from the dead, gone back to fishing, all because of his sin. And on it goes. The base sin for these – and me – was the same: either a lack of trust in God and His Word or a love of other things more than God. The stories of these men are written so that it does not have to be so with us. And I write to you, my child, that you do not repeat the sins of your father, but that you would heed the warnings in this very testimony.

Paul would speak of the sins of his life in generalities, in words that lead us to understand the sin and the pain. Dr. Luke, in his Acts of the Apostles, gives us part of the picture with the story of Saul consenting to the death of Stephen as the witnesses' clothes were laid at his feet. We know, in general, about his persecutions of the saints. But do we know the fullness, the details? We read in his words to Timothy at Ephesus:

'I thank him who has given me strength, Christ Jesus our Lord, because he judged me faithful, appointing me to his service, though formerly I was a blasphemer, persecutor, and insolent opponent. But I received mercy because I had acted ignorantly in unbelief' (1 Tim. 1:12-13).

As Paul refrained from such things, I must. Out of fear? No. Out of shame? Surely. Out of concealment? Hardly. Public records of the courts tell so much. But let me say this as a record of this testimony: I will never forget the day I walked out of my Aunt Eva's house and was married at seventeen years of age (by only one month). The day I left home, my Aunt Eva told me, 'Son, you will come home again, but it will be as a broken man.' I will never forget her words, for they came true. I was repeating the sins of my father.

From the days of my adolescence through the early years of my twenties, I led a life of waywardness from God. At the conclusion of that time, I knew of my sin and began to seek to return to God, though the way home took many turns. At the conclusion of my prodigal journey in the far country of sin and shame, I went back home to her and laid my head on her lap and cried. I was a broken man.

During the years between the time I left Aunt Eva's home and the time I returned to her, there were great struggles, great sins – and I guess if I named them all, I would hit on at least one of your besetting sins today. But my worse sin was unbelief. But there was also grace in the midst of sin. Before I was twenty, I was father to two daughters – both of them deaf. Then, God would bring a son, also profoundly deaf. But that being said, their deafness was not and is not the thing that defines them. I think that what defines these three remarkable human beings is their strength and hope despite all of the odds. They became a great light in my life.[1] At length, I would lose even them, lose fatherhood (how I was reunited with them is a story unto itself, and I will get to that story soon). Losing them was just part of life in the far country. The story need not be retold here, but for many years I would be driven to my knees in prayer and utter brokenness before God over these losses. How great was my loss in that far country.

Do you dare think, my child, that you can cash in your inheritance and run to live life apart from God when you have already known of Him? Shall you trample on the very blood of the Lord Jesus and ignore His atonement for you? Having had the saintly hand of my Aunt Eva laid on my head as a child, I was sinning against both God *and*

---

[1] I will not use their names and will leave them to recognize themselves as I write.

[2] The song, 'Down the Road,' was written about this time in my life (see Michael Anthony Milton, 'Down the Road,' *He Shall Restore* (Music for Missions compact disc recording, released December 2005, copyright Michael Anthony Milton and Music for Missions).

her as I went on my journey.[2] My life bears witness to the unimaginable pain that sin brings.

What God said of Israel, he meant for me and all like me:

> 'But if you or your sons turn away from me and do not observe the commands and decrees I have given you and go off to serve other gods and worship them, then I will cut off Israel from the land I have given them and will reject this temple I have consecrated for my Name. Israel will then become a byword and an object of ridicule among all peoples. And though this temple is now imposing, all who pass by will be appalled and will scoff and say, "Why has the LORD done such a thing to this land and to this temple?"' (1 Kings 9:6-8 NIV).

And my beloved child, my dear reader, loving lamb of God under my pastoral care, shall you not also bring ruin to your own soul and your life and your family by going against the will of God when you now know better? But He is a gracious God:

> 'If my people, who are called by my name, will humble themselves and pray and seek my face and turn from their wicked ways, then will I hear from heaven and will forgive their sin and will heal their land' (2 Chron. 7:14 NIV).

> 'Repent therefore, and turn again, that your sins may be blotted out' (Acts 3:19).

I must say no more of this. I was a failure in so many ways and I am not the least bit interested in casting stones. I dare not, lest God show me my own wickedness in this matter.

Let me say this much: I know what it means to be a prodigal son. I know what it means to be in the far country. When Jesus told the story of the lost coin, the lost sheep, and then 'upped the ante' by telling the story of the 'lost boy' – or 'the prodigal son' as it is called most often – I knew what he was talking about. I was that boy. But of course, in the story of the 'lost boy,' the boy comes to his senses, which is a grace unto itself, and he decides to return to his father's house. But isn't the greatest grace in the story the grace of a heart-broken father who runs to meet the son? Until that moment, the prodigal boy is not really acting out of grace, but despair. True grace, saving grace, is bound up in the Father who takes the initiative to welcome the lost boy and claim him as a son.

That is what I want to tell you next.

7

Grace in the Hog Pen

> 'Sin is the death of the soul. A man dead in trespasses and sins has no desire for spiritual pleasures. When we look upon a corpse, it gives an awful feeling. A never-dying spirit is now fled, and has left nothing but the ruins of a man. But if we viewed things aright, we should be far more affected by the thought of a dead soul, a lost, fallen spirit' (Matthew Henry).
>
> 'But God demonstrates his own love for us in this: While we were still sinners, Christ died for us' (Rom. 5:8).

God was so good to me while I was in the hog pen. Like that prodigal son – that lost boy – I squandered all I had very quickly. And I lost so much: Aunt Eva's name and good teaching, her trust, the trust of others; in fact, I didn't trust myself. The Bible says that the lost boy came to his senses. The truth is, though, that boy still didn't know of his father's grace until he came all the way home. In fact, he wasn't sure what would happen. He had hoped, at best, to get a job as a hired hand, so to speak. If he could just live as they lived, he would be better off than he was. No self-respecting

Jewish boy would like to have been in his condition, having to scratch out an existence in a hog pen. This wasn't just any animal, it was the symbol of ritual uncleanness, a swine! Well, as I said, he hadn't yet seen his father's response. He just came to his senses and knew this sad chapter was over.

I first began to think about the possibility of turning pages, to think about another chapter in my life story, one night in San Angelo, Texas. I was there because I was in the Navy Security Group with a Top Secret clearance. I was an Albanian interpreter. I had just graduated from the Defense Language Institute in Monterey, California, and had been transferred for training in cryptology at the United States Air Force School of Applied Cryptological Science, Goodfellow Air Force Base, San Angelo. On that night after studying, I was all alone in my room. I had a cigarette burning, another pack smoked away. I had no money in my pocket, having to borrow money from others to eat, but somehow I had a bottle of whiskey sitting in front of me. It was mostly full, because I didn't like the taste of the stuff. In fact, I never liked the taste of alcoholic beverages. I think I drank because I secretly wanted to be my father. Well, I was turning into him all right. My life was falling apart, and at that time, I was not yet nineteen years old. I remember writing something like this in a journal I kept:

> 'I know that God has something for me, but not this. I just don't know how to get from here to wherever that is.'

It is important for me to take a break here to tell you about the jobs I held both just prior to that time and after. I want to tell you because it shows, not amazing vocational breadth and depth, but a lost soul trying to find himself. How much better it is to follow God early in life.

When I was still in school, I had been a political cartoonist. I drew for the Denham Springs News. I did weekly editorial cartoons. I met with the editor each week and he told me what he wanted – usually local politics – but occasionally he would let me 'have at' President Richard Nixon's Watergate mess, which I greatly enjoyed. Like any other boy, I had a variety of summer jobs. I worked at a ranch and camp where I did everything from mending fences to training horses to being a lifeguard. One time I was a janitor for the school board in a summer program developed for underprivileged youth. After I left Aunt Eva's house, I worked as a pest control man, and a door-to-door salesman who sold everything from electric signs to photograph albums.

I thought I had really hit it big when I moved up to life insurance. In a way, I guess I had. But all of that happened in a course of just a year or so. I was moving from job to job and I began to see enough of the world, at not quite eighteen, to know that I could never realize Aunt Eva's dream of seeing me educated and out of our poor lifestyle without, of course, an education. That is what led me to seek out the opportunities in the U.S. Navy. In fact, I took a test to qualify for the school and work that I wanted in the Navy, and then set off for boot camp in San Diego. I will never regret serving my country as I did. I will always be thankful for the start that the Navy gave me in my education. I applied to and was accepted into the Defense Language Institute (DLI) of Monterey, California. This is the world famous language training school that trains linguists for our military as well as for other agencies of our government. I was selected to study Albanian. As far as I knew, I had never met nor heard an Albanian. Today when I tell people that I studied Albanian in college, they look at me funny and ask, 'But why Albanian?' My answer is simple: 'The United States Navy said so. Period.'

For five and six days per week for about a year, I studied the language and history and customs of the people of ancient Illyria under a top secret clearance. One night at the enlisted club at the Presidio of Monterey, I was asked that question, and I remember answering with blaspheming, 'I don't know why in G-d's name I am learning this ___ language!' Little did I know that exactly fourteen years later, I would stand in Skenderberg Square in Tirana, the Albanian capital, and preach the Gospel of Jesus Christ while standing on the fallen statue of Enver Hoxha (the dictator of Albania during Communism).[1] There is an old saying where I come from about eating the 'whole hog' and not leaving a thing! Well, God uses our whole experience. Every joy I had, as well as every sorrow, every experience, was fashioned by this sovereign and good God into making me His son and making me useful for His glorious plan. Thus we read,

> 'For by grace you have been saved through faith. And this is not your own doing; it is the gift of God, not a result of works, so that no one may boast. **For we are his workmanship, created in Christ Jesus for good works, which God prepared beforehand, that we should walk in them** [*my emphasis*]' (Eph. 2:8-10).

I think often of these days and draw from the characters, events, mistakes and even sorrows of sin to illustrate the truth of Scripture when I preach.

The Lord impresses me now, even as I write, to encourage you, my child. May the Lord give you spiritual eyes to see His hand moving over the events of your life. May you be given spiritual ears to hear His footsteps in your moments of trial. May you be given a spiritual mind to comprehend the truth of His sovereignty, which brings hope.

It would be some years before I could understand this sovereign grace. I left the active duty of the Navy early, under hardship, in order to care for my deaf children – pulling them around the world would be difficult, given their challenge and the inevitable challenges of schooling. I returned to Louisiana – not an idea I relished – and after

---

[1] I once remarked in a sermon that I stood on the crumbled remains of Joseph Stalin. But on a recent, second, trip to Albania, I was told that the statue was actually of Hoxha. The Albanian who told me this then said, 'Eshte ma mere!' ('This is even better!).

some other odd jobs, I was invited to work in the oil fields of South Louisiana for Dow Chemical. It was hard work and long hours doing some of the most physical work I have ever done: rigging pipe from a pump truck to the oil well. We would sleep under the pipe racks and for days on end would be available twenty-four hours per day to go to work. It was usually hot, sticky, and tedious, alternating at once between boredom and life-threatening danger. One time, I was back at the Dow Chemical plant, waiting for another job to come in and doing janitorial work, when I saw a fellow walk in with a clean, white shirt, a tie, and shiny shoes. I asked, 'What does that fellow do?' The guy next to me replied, 'He is a salesman.' I rubbed my chin, and thought, 'Well, that is what I want to do.' My buddy informed me that one had to have a college degree to get that job. I said, 'Well, I have about two years worth of college from DLI (the language school).' I had that and ambition. After about a year, I was made a salesman, calling on oil wells in South Louisiana, around Morgan City and Houma.

My personal life was shameful, but ambition and a God-given gift to cast a vision of 'what could be' if the company representative bought my product, caused me to shoot up like a star in the organization. Isn't that the way some of you feel? Your business is going great, even as your family is disintegrating before you. Your organization is showering you with accolades while your relationship with your children grows colder. How do we get into these messes? In a word, sin. I cannot begin to tell you how the unanswered questions of my life continued to eat away at me like a parasite.

> 'And he was longing to be fed with the pods that the pigs ate, and no one gave him anything' (Luke 15:16).

I ate, I slept, and I worked. And I died over and over again in so many ways.

Meanwhile the Spirit of God hovered over the deep, dark chaos of my soul, and He would soon begin His re-creative work in my life. How He came to awaken me is the subject of my next chapter.

8

I Will Arise and Go to My Father

> 'In short, all the miseries which we endure are a profitable invitation to repentance' (John Calvin).

> 'But when he came to himself, he said, "How many of my father's hired servants have more than enough bread, but I perish here with hunger! I will arise and go to my father, and I will say to him, 'Father, I have sinned against heaven and against you'"' (Luke 15:17-18).

I remember driving down the winding roads of South Louisiana, under the canopy of Live Oaks and moss and cypress trees, on both sides banked by swamp. I was making sales calls on oil wells down there. The driving gave me a lot of time to think. I was thinking that my life was a long way from the faith that Aunt Eva had prayed for me. The days of hearing her teaching, bowing with her hand on my head, seemed like a sweet but far away dream. During these days I listened to Christian radio. I would hear D. James Kennedy, Charles Stanley, Charles Swindoll, J. Vernon McGee, and others (including some outside of the pale of orthodoxy). I became burdened about being in the hog pen of life. I waned to return to the Father's House. But how?

During one of my sales calls on a Tuesday morning in Morgan City, Louisiana, I was so burdened that I had to find a minister or someone to express my heart to and to find the way home. I was thinking about how my life was so messed up and how Aunt Eva had taught me better, when all of a sudden I came across a sign: 'Morning Prayer at 10:30 on Tuesdays.' It was a small Episcopal church. I did not think twice. I pulled over, and like a man rushing into the emergency room, I rushed into that church! I paused, caught my breath, and took in the scene. In this small, rather ordinary looking sanctuary, there was the vicar, what I assumed was his wife, one other lady (a rather older woman), and me. I sat down in my own pew. The liturgy started. I had never been in an Episcopal church before, and while the 'ups and downs' were different to me, I could hear the Bible in the Morning Prayer service. Between the sonorous voice of this small-town vicar, talking a bit louder than usual to drown out the coughing of the window air conditioner unit, and my own thoughts condemning me, I came to understand that I was a sinner. In fact, I will always remember his text:

> 'And whoever does not take his cross and follow me is not worthy of me' (Matt. 10:38).

I did not completely understand, at that moment, what it meant to take up the cross. I did not fully understand or assent to what the cross of Christ meant. I knew that I was far from God, but I did not know how far until that service. I was not following Jesus Christ, that was for certain. So those few words, read by the minister that day, cut deep into my soul like a surgeon's knife. The words exposed my spiritual condition. I believe the Holy Spirit, on that morning, showed me my sin. But I still had far to go to get home.

Sometimes we think of the conversion experience as a single occurrence, happening all at once – a man sees his sin, repents of it, and comes to the Lord. That happens. But it also happens, especially with covenant children, that we see our sin, desire forgiveness, and seek it over time through repentance, faith, and trust in the finished work of Jesus Christ. This is what happened to me. It is also what happened in Jesus' story about the lost boy.

> 'When he came to his senses, he said, "How many of my father's hired men have food to spare, and here I am starving to death! I will set out and go back to my father and say to him: 'Father, I have sinned against heaven and against you. I am no longer worthy to be called your son; make me like one of your hired men'"' (Luke 15:17-19 NIV).

You can see the situation: the lost boy is tired of the sad story of his life. He is tired of the hog pods. He wants home, and he wonders about his father. He has a poor understanding of his father's love, for this boy says, 'Make me like one of your hired hands.' In other words, 'I will do whatever it takes to come home.'

Have you ever been gone from your home for a long time and you longingly sighed, almost with tears in your eyes, and moaned, 'I just want to go home.' 'Home' has such a ring to it. That is what I desired so much. 'Home' was the place where the Word of God healed me, where God was near, where Christ was real to me, where I was not under the wrath of God but under His mercy.

I had wasted so much, and I had infected so many other people with my sin. There was no time to waste. I had to go home. When I say this, I am saying that immediately I began to take steps to get home – as if I could make that trip in my own strength, and as if I really knew the way home. I didn't. But I rushed forward. I not only smelled like a hog pen, if you will – that is, my sin in my life and in my relationships was still so much a part of me – but I even scooped up the pods and slop and brought it with me. 'I had decided to follow Jesus' as the little song goes. But that decision was still filled with a fleshly understanding of who I was and who God is and how I could get to Him.

The way home, for me, took many winding paths. It started with religion. That is the way it works for desperate refugee sons seeking asylum from the consequences of sin. But is trading the 'far country' for a 'negotiated peace' really how to know His grace?

9

Filthy Rags

> 'See what ruin sin brings upon a people; and an outward profession of holiness will be no defense against it' (Matthew Henry).
>
> 'All of us have become like one who is unclean, and all our righteous acts are like filthy rags; we all shrivel up like a leaf, and like the wind our sins sweep us away' (Isa. 64:6).

'Well,' I thought, 'I will just have to get back in church.' That was the road I chose to take in order to make my way back home to God. That was my 'negotiated peace' with the God of grace. What that meant, practically, was getting involved with a church. I originally had thought that since awareness of my sin condition had occurred in an Episcopal Church, I would start there. But that was not to be, so I chose the Methodist Church. I chose a congregation, not based on preaching or teaching or doctrine or anything that I would count as important today, but just because it was Methodist. The Miltons had been Methodists before, so why not?

I had not been in church regularly since I was a child under Aunt Eva's tutelage, and it was all rather new to me. Another thing that was new was the emphasis on the mechanisms of the church rather than on the teachings of the Lord. I intuitively recognized the difference between what I witnessed in the particular congregation I chose and the faith of Aunt Eva, but I internalized it, didn't deal with it, and went forward. I embraced the idea of God without embracing God. I embraced a philosophy of Christianity without embracing Christ. I embraced a religion about Jesus rather than a relationship with Jesus. I was not a disciple of Jesus. I was a disciple of the Methodist church. That is not a black mark on the Methodist church – John Wesley would have seen right through the farce of my confession since he, himself, had been a hypocrite and a washed up missionary in Savannah, Georgia. Nor is it an indictment of any other person but me. I had been reared to know better than this.

At this point, I did know that I was in the hog pen, that I had to get home to the Father's house. The route I took led me towards home, but not to home. In fact, I went into a new sort of far country. And do you know what? Life changed very little in my relationships. In fact, I was even more miserable because now, being in church, I had to keep up the appearance that all was all right. But, of course, it wasn't.

In the midst of this period of my life, I decided that if 'one scoop is good, two scoops must be better.' I decided, in my twisted thinking, that if I could please God through being involved in a church, then if I became a lay preacher in that church, that would be an even greater badge of honor. I secretly felt that I was not only pleasing God, but also pleasing Aunt Eva. So I became, through about six Saturday morning lessons, a certified lay preacher in the United Methodist Church. I would go and help out wherever I was needed. Well, a dying congregation in a declining neighborhood in Baton Rouge needed help. So, I went. Still working at Dow Chemical (actually, my career was going very well indeed) I moved into their pastor's residence and began to help them. I was there, I think, for about three months. I worked very hard at trying to encourage them, to get them working for renewal, and at the same time I was working in South Louisiana, in Houma and Morgan City. But my life and relationships were increasingly complex and difficult. I shall say no more on this, pleading the Scriptural honesty and modesty which announces sin but goes no further. But let me say that my life spiraled downward. In a matter of months since I had learned, in that little Episcopal Church, that I was a sinner and needed to come home, I had tried and gone the wrong way. I was embarrassed and thought more about that than anything. I was still so far from God. One day, alone now, I packed up my things in my car, and drove to Aunt Eva's place. I laid my head down on her lap and I cried – for a long time, I cried. Why and how I got there is of importance to some, but not to this book.

My child, let me say only a word about the most important relationship in life, this side of a relationship with Jesus Christ, and that is marriage. I know the blessings of marriage. It is God's great gift that forms the very cornerstone of our society. I have known the brokenness of failure that chips away at that stone. And let me speak directly to the dissolution of the Covenant of Marriage.

Divorce, whether it is on biblical grounds or not, whether it happens when you are not following the Lord or, God forbid, when you are, is less like a chipping away at a cornerstone, and is more like a nuclear bomb detonating. As the bomb goes off, it sends its shock waves through the lives of others, even through generations. The deadly radiation of the dissolution of the Covenant of Marriage infects the souls of those closest to the detonation point. Its ungodly power is such that it extends in deadly and unexpected ways to generation after generation, then and there, as well as across time. It is not without reason, then, that we read that God hates divorce. It destroys the well-intended life He has planned for the family of man because it is not His best will for us. Divorce, even when regulated by God's Word, leaves gashes in the human soul that need to be filled with the healing power of God's grace. It is only through God's grace in Jesus Christ, only through redemption in Him, that new life can spring from the aftermath. It is only through Jesus Christ that a new covenant can cover the sins, provide the purity of life that is needed to go forward. I thank God that if you are in that condition and you are reading this book, you, too, can know that healing. As one of the broken people of our generation who now, by the grace of God, pastors others under the Lordship of the one true Shepherd, I invite you to open your heart to receive and give true, total forgiveness. It comes from the cross where Jesus died for your sins. And it flows through you and into the lives of others – your ex-wife or ex-husband, your parents, your children, the other man, the other woman, those who said what they shouldn't have and those who did not speak. God's love covers a multitude of sins. God's love creates new hope out of the hopeless, barren ground that divorce leaves. My beloved child, there is no situation is life so far gone that Christ Jesus and the power of His redeeming love cannot reach it. For in going to the far reaches of loneliness and despair, on the cross, He now can find you very easily. Through His life and death and resurrection, and through faith in Him, you have access to an eternal hope that changes everything.

I did not have that new hope when I pulled into Aunt Eva's driveway. And Aunt Eva, of course, knew it. She told me, 'Son, you are not where you ought to be in your life. You are missing something. And all I know is that God has started something in you, and He will complete it. For what God starts, God finishes. Turn to Him, Mike. Turn to the Lord and trust in Him. He now has you right where He wants you, but you must turn to Him. Right now you are not there.'

She was patient, and she was kind. I hope that as I come across people who are in the far country, trying to find their way home, I will remember how Aunt Eva guided me. I not only pray that I can model Aunt Eva's patience, I pray that I will be as patient with others as God was with me. God is the father who waits on His children. He loves them. He draws them home with His love. He puts up with foolish children who don't understand His grace.

I had left home at sixteen; ignored all wisdom and entered a relationship at seventeen that brought pain to so many; was a father of three deaf children by twenty-two; worked in numerous jobs, including a top secret position with the US Navy; graduated from the Defense Language Institute; worked for Dow Chemical and moved from a laborer to an executive salesman in New Orleans; started and failed as a lay preacher and 'religious' person; and moved back home with Aunt Eva.

My life was broken in pieces. The only thing not damaged was my work, where I was able to channel the energy of the pain into the job. But soon I would be a single father; a hopeless creature still seeking approval from men and from God by my own actions; and a young man increasingly given to the vices of the world to medicate my failures. I even began to think about suicide.

I had become, at last, my father.

10

Mae

> 'See what ruin sin brings upon a people; and an outward profession of holiness will be no defense against it' (Matthew Henry).
>
> 'A wife of noble character who can find? She is worth far more than rubies' (Prov. 31:10).

Mae was my father's wife's name. As I have written, she was not my mother; she was the childless first wife of Ellis Milton. She was faithful when he was faithless. She kept his name with honor when he foolishly ruined it (I thank God that by his repentance and faith, he renewed the honor of his name and memory). Mae. The name which I had heard secretly mentioned in conversations between my aunts – always spoken with tenderness – became a name that would come into my heart and change me. How amazing that the same name, the name of my father's wife (who died not too long ago), would be the name of my wife too. And I must say this: as President Ronald Reagan was known to say that 'Nancy saved my soul,' so I say that of my wife, Mae. Mae saved me. I do not mean, any more than President Reagan meant, that a woman literally saved my soul from eternal separation from God, but that Mae, like Nancy Reagan had done for the late President, brought hope and even right thinking to my life. She was used of God to help me find a way home to God. When I even say her name now, I experience – and I do not exaggerate – a sense of calm, peace, security, and hope. I smile when I say her name. I knew these feelings from Aunt Eva. And I know these feelings from Mae. She is the gift of God to me. I shall bless the name of Christ Jesus for the name of Mae. In a real way, she held my one hand, Aunt Eva held my other, and together they led me from the forest next to the land of grace into the open arms of Jesus Christ. They were His beautiful guides, ordained by the Lord to bring me Home. This is how I think of Mae, my partner in life and in ministry.

And how did we meet? I have often heard of the most beautiful and romantic ways in which couples met – in a Sunday school class or in a small group or on a beach or even today through places like eHarmony.com! How we came to be is part of, not only our romantic story, but of course, the very story of our lives. As a pastor I ask that question. My relationship with my wife started as friends. We ended up looking to each other for help as our lives, individually, were being consumed with pain and sorrow. So, I cannot say that we met in an ideal situation. If such a couple came before me today, I would have great concern for them. However, future bliss sometimes comes to us when we are in the worst places in our lives. Some men find their wives as they are nursed back to health, recovering from wounds in warfare. That is a metaphor that is about as close to the truth as I can find for how we met. As our friendship began to evolve, I found the most gracious, kind, tender, and precious person I have ever known, other than Aunt Eva. I brought her to see my Aunt Eva as we were moving into a time of courtship. Afterward Aunt Eva told me that she would pray for Mae to be my wife. She believed that this woman was my future. I agreed, but neither of us could go in that direction at that point. My life was coming unglued from my life in the far country. It was as if bombs were going off and shrapnel was flying, like the world was being lived in black and white, and then, in the midst of the battle, in taking cover, I found a beautiful orchid, in full color, growing next to the place where I had fallen. Mae was – is – that orchid.

Life was good and life was hard; life was complicated and life was clear; life was hopeless and life was hopeful. But in the midst of it all, there was Mae.

My wife was a single mother of four when we married. Mae had grown up as a Methodist preacher's daughter – one of four daughters – in Southern Illinois. Her father had been a coal miner. He was converted under the preaching of a holiness Methodist evangelist. As is the case with some, this man surrendered to the call to preach almost simultaneously with God's call to salvation. Floyd Slow went to seminary and began to pastor congregations in the rural communities and small towns of Southern Illinois.

Mae was born in Galatia, Illinois, in the manse next to a typical midwestern white clapboard church, placed, as if by God Himself, in the midst of a great cornfield. The pastoral family moved every three years or so. Mae lived in many homes, went to several different schools, and seemed to always be the new kid in school. The Rev. Floyd Slow died when Mae was thirteen years of age. Her mother, Elsie, Mae, and her sister Tina (the other two sisters were older and already out of the home) had to move from the manse but had nowhere to go. One of the hardest things in the life of churches is what to do with a former pastor's widow and children. Because of what happened to Mae and her family, we have a great heart for the plight of pastoral families who find themselves in hard situations, all because they surrendered to preach the Gospel and serve the flock of Christ. In Mae's case, they all moved in with her grandfather. He died a year later, leaving the home to Elsie. My mother-in-law worked hard for the rest of her life, until the last years that she spent with us here in Chattanooga. She took care of others – the elderly, the infirmed, the disabled. Most often her care involved changing bedpans and hand feeding those who could not feed themselves. She did what she could to take care of her girls. She did her best, but her best still left two girls growing up with little.

For the rest of Mae's growing up years, she was poor, malnourished, and usually alone. But she was steady and reliable and pretty and – she was always this – sweet. There is no word for Mae other than just – pardon the Southernness – 'plain old sweet.' Her smile and her eyes speak of a soul that knows no malice, harbors no resentments, keeps no prisoners. Her laughter is the laughter of a child. Her wisdom is the rare but real wisdom one finds in the Midwest of our United States – plain, no nonsense, simple – just the opposite of my own thinking – muddle-headed, grandiose, and as murky as the swamps of South Louisiana. Mae, as a teenager, sought a way out of her poverty. She went to live with her sister, who was by that time living in Louisiana, and ended up staying. I met her there, many years later. She, too, was living in a 'black and white' world caused by abuse and divorce. Yet, as I watched her, she – almost naively – smiled. In the midst of devastation, she smiled, and orchids bloomed in the midst of war.

I will say this now: I loved her then, but I did not love her as much as I love her today. I was not then, as I am not now, as wise as she. Nor am I as deeply spiritual. Her wisdom and spirituality are formed in a purer soul than mine. The blisters of the pain of the past have left marks – like smallpox marks – on my soul. Yet her soul seems less affected by those things and able to see things more clearly. I am like a spiritual amputee who must lean against her. It was that way then, too. Mae saw that our situation was hard. I asked her to marry me as we were parked in a car in front of a grocery store, trapped by a sudden downpour – again, not exactly the beach or the mountains. But since it was raining outside and we couldn't get out of the car to go in the store, I thought, 'Why wait to do this at dinner?' Romantic moments are not made by the surroundings: the moments transform the surroundings into something special. So, I asked her to marry me. She waited to give me the final answer for some time. I went to her mother and asked her and she consented – with joy, I might add. We did not have the blessing of pastoral counsel. Therefore, we were navigating the possibility of a 'blended family' marriage without a compass.

During this time, we joined, individually, the Episcopal Church. We were confirmed on the same day at St. James Episcopal Church in Baton Rouge, Louisiana. That church and her ministers, especially the godly 'Father Coleman,' began to be used of God to turn our hearts toward home. I say 'our' because Mae had been reared, as mentioned, in a holiness Wesleyan background. She took away from that a sense of having to work to earn your salvation. The concept of an 'entire sanctification' in this life seemed far removed from reality. Thus, as Mae and I joined our hearts together, we were both in a far country, needing to get home to the front porch of God's grace. During our time of worshiping in the Episcopal Church, we experienced a sense of healing, of being washed and cleansed by the Word of the Lord coming through the liturgy of the *Book of Common Prayer*. We looked forward each Sunday to the services. I remember the warmth of the presence of the Lord calling me, working in me, and wooing me to Himself. During those days, I came to realize the emptiness of religion and the power of God's Word in worship. It is a power that to this day gives me strength for living. John Stott has called such power in worship, 'living worship.' I truly believe that God was there with us in those days. Though I still did not fully comprehend God's grace, nor had I yielded my life in obedience to God, I knew He was there.

This thought has come to me many times as I have ministered the Gospel as a pastor. I am often preaching to people who are there in the seats in church, but they are on a pilgrimage. At any given time in a service, I am preaching – remembering the story, again, of the 'lost boy' and the good father – to those desiring to 'cash in' their spiritual inheritance in order to go into the world. I am also preaching to those who are already there and are deluded into believing that such living will give them more than a temporary thrill, when in fact they are like swine, eating and enjoying their slop, all the while on the way to the slaughter house! Then there are those who are in the pigpen. The money is gone. The thrill is gone. They are alone. They are backslidden and are paying the price of sin. There are those who have 'come to their senses' and desire to go to the Father, but they don't understand the Father's love. They wonder if they can 'work it off' like a hired hand – and that is what I believed. They wonder if they will be received at all. Then there are those who have left the pigpen, and they are trying to find a way home. Perhaps, like me, they have taken the wrong road to get there, but they want to go home. My work, as pastor, is to preach the Gospel of Jesus Christ, whether I am in Genesis or Revelation, whether in the pulpit or the hospital room, in season and out of season. I have come to know, fully and without equivocation, that this 'Word from Another World' (as Dr. Robert L. Reymond puts it) is powerful enough to meet each of those people at each of their unique stations in life.

During these Sundays at the Episcopal Church, our hearts continued to grow together. I wanted an answer. I was, at this time, working as an executive sales representative out of New Orleans. I was doing quite a bit of traveling around the country, calling on corporate accounts. Whereas at one time I used to be the laborer who connected the heavy iron pipes to bring the chemicals into the well bore of the hole, I was now the man who sold the chemicals to major oil companies. I thank God for those days.

Despite the pain, the losses, the fears, and the tales of practical unbelief, my life was soothed by Mae. When I finally moved away from Aunt Eva's home to live near

New Orleans where I worked, I would drive to see Mae in the afternoons, visit with her, eat dinner, and then leave to return to New Orleans. It was about a four-hour round trip journey several times per week, and that kept up for a year. I wondered whether she would answer my proposal.

One day, as I was driving along Interstate 12, I pulled off the road and went to a nearby pharmacy to get some aspirin. While there, I spotted a payphone (these were the days before we all had cell phones). My heart began beating faster within my chest. I wanted to call her and ask her again. 'Should I?' I wondered. I turned on my heels, leaving the entrance to the drug store, and walked with a fast, deliberate pace toward the pay phone. I called Mae's workplace. She answered. We chit-chatted. I then asked, 'Have you thought any more about my proposal?' What a foolish question. Of course, she would have thought about it! It was the biggest thing in our lives. There was silence. Mae then told me, 'Yes, I have thought about it.' My heart stopped for that split second. 'Yes, I will marry you.' I let out a yell that almost got me arrested! I thanked her and told her that I would do all I could to be a good husband or something like that. I honestly can't remember anything else but ecstasy. After we finished our call, I yelled again, and in my exuberance, I forgot to put the phone on the receiver. I saw it hanging, rushed back, put the phone on the hook, and yelled again. I left to tell Aunt Eva. I never did get that aspirin.

We were married in Tennessee. Given all that we had been through, and given that Tennessee was about equal distance between her home state of Illinois and mine, it worked out nicely. A Baptist minister married us in a chapel not that far from where we live now. After we were married, we honeymooned in the Great Smoky Mountains. I remember walking by the Pigeon Forge River, taking in the beauty of the whole area, and remarking to my bride, 'We will live here one day.'

We returned to Louisiana and held a reception for the immediate family. We were off and running, but there were some big things ahead of us, and we had few resources to deal with them – things like, how do we lead a blended family? how do we help children make this adjustment? how do we build a marriage while doing all of that? During this time, I also suffered the reality of the loss of children. They had been brought into another family, with another man, another life. I had *de facto* lost them. It remained only to accept the inevitable. I would not have contact with them again for more than a decade. This would become the greatest loss of my life. It would break my heart a million times and then break it again. But it would ultimately drive me to my knees and teach me prayer. O. Hallesby wrote,

> 'I never grow tired of emphasizing our helplessness, for it is the decisive factor not only in our prayer life, but in our whole relationship to God.'

And so it was, and is, with me.

By this time, we had purchased a home in Prairieville, Louisiana. There was no Episcopal Church there so we decided to join a local Baptist congregation. We had our pick. On a three-mile road, there were three Baptist churches, all originally from the same group! As for the leap from Anglicanism to Baptist, it may seem like a big jump, but I had been reared Baptist. Having gone on such a denominational journey before, it didn't seem that big a deal going to yet another one. One thing is for sure: I was not yet my Master's disciple. I was a churchgoer – a knowledgeable churchgoer – but not yet a disciple. I am thankful that God's Spirit drew me even there, for I was sitting under the preaching of the Word. It is better for an unbeliever to be hearing the Word than not hearing the Word. Of course, it can be to his own destruction if he does not heed the call to Christ. But God can also use those times to cultivate the cold ground of unbelief in order to raise up a great crop of faith.

I remember that the minister there, a fine man of God named Dr. Nathan Luce, asked me to teach a class. I was hesitant, given my failure as a lay preacher. I told him he had the wrong man, but he won, and I taught. Again, it must seem incongruent – and it should be – that a man who is not a true disciple of the Master should be teaching about Him. But it is easy to teach about Jesus and abhor the Bible. Many others have done it. It is not that difficult to memorize the texts of Scripture, imitate a preacher's communication style, or even invite someone to receive Jesus as Lord. You can watch it being modeled for you any time on television. In my case, I saw it growing up. There is a certain rhythm, a certain way. Charles Finney, in the *Second Great Awakening*, perfected the methodologies of revival in his book of the same name. This is what I was doing.

Dr. Luce then came to me and asked me a question: 'Have you ever heard of Dr. D. James Kennedy?' I said that I had. I listened to his 'Truths that Transform' radio program in my car each day as I drove to make sales calls on the oil wells. 'Well, Dr. Kennedy has an evangelism equipping ministry called Evangelism Explosion. A clinic is coming to New Orleans next month. Mike, I want you to use a week's vacation, go down there, get equipped to go out and share the Gospel, then teach others.' I told him, again, 'Dr. Luce, you have the wrong man.' 'No, Mike, I have the man God has led me to ask. I challenge you to go.' My decision to accept that challenge became one of the most important decisions of my life. Had I said 'no' to Dr. Luce ... well, I don't want to even think about it! One of the ways that decision was made was through a strong layman in the church named Charles Marceux. Charles was a neighbor. One afternoon he dropped by for a visit as I was outside splitting firewood.

'Mike, Dr. Luce told me about his invitation.'

'Well, it was more like a challenge.'

'Yea, he gave it to me, too. Mike, I really believe that you ought to go. I am going and I want you to be with me. And Mike – one more thing – I want to give you this.'

He handed me a Gideon New Testament. I held it in my hand. I had known the Scriptures, taught them, preached them as a lay preacher, and even shared them with others.

'Charles, why don't you give this to someone who needs it?'

'Mike, I think I just have. Open the front.'

In the front, he had written my name and his. Something about that touched me instantly.

'Charles, I will go.'

I told Mae. She smiled the smile of contentment. Somehow she knew this was what was needed in my life.

I wanted desperately, now, not to infect others with my pain. For I was only twenty-six, only ten years away from rebellion emanating from unanswered questions and, yet, had been through so much. By this time I was frightened that I would mess things up again.

Frightened, confused, broken, and yet happy with the best wife a man ever could have, I accepted the challenge to go to Evangelism Explosion. It was a decision that changed my life for eternity.

11

The Grace that Got Me Home

'Candles receive their light from what they are not; Men, grace from Him, for whom at first they care not' (John Bunyan).

'For by grace are ye saved through faith; and that not of yourselves: it is the gift of God' (Eph. 2:8 KJV).

The things that come against you in the hands of a loving God become the very things that lead you to God. That was my experience.

I took my place on the first day of this Evangelism Explosion clinic at a Baptist Church in New Orleans, Louisiana (the place of my first and now second birth). I sat there, and the leader spoke and gave an overview of our course for the coming week. It seemed daunting to me. Then, a tape was played of Dr. D. James Kennedy presenting the Gospel of Jesus Christ. He asked those famous questions that have now been used the world over:

'If you were to die today, and you were to stand before God, and He were to ask you, "Why should I let you into My heaven?" What would you say?'

> 'If God were to ask you, "Why should I let you into My heaven?" How would you respond?'

Dr. Kennedy then proceeded to speak on God's grace, man's condition, God's love and His justice, Christ's Person and sacrifice, the gift of faith, and a personal challenge to repent and transfer trust completely to Jesus Christ.

By the time he quoted Ephesians 2:8-9[1] I was spiritually arrested, tried, and found guilty of self-righteousness, and yet so crushed that I knew all I wanted was His forgiveness and grace. I prayed to receive Him by grace in my heart right then, with words I cannot remember, but words which shot up in my heart, silently, like a geyser erupting from years of searching and a lifetime of pain. In a moment, in the twinkling of an eye, Jesus Christ broke through the fog of my thinking, the darkness of my soul, the deadness of my heart, to bring me His truth. His truth is that we are saved by grace, through faith, and that not of ourselves. From that one passage, spoken by Dr. D. James Kennedy through a recording at an Evangelism Explosion clinic, my life, my eternal destiny, my world changed. And even the word 'changed' seems so pedestrian, common. I saw Jesus alive in my life for the first time.

Lost in the wonder of new life suddenly appearing, I was given the ability by God to hear Dr. Kennedy's final words, dealing with the essence of genuine discipleship – the Bible, prayer, worship, fellowship, and witness – and I became aware that I had never been a true disciple of Jesus. Even when I was a 'lay preacher' working to earn my salvation, I was in no way His true disciple. But in that instant, I wanted more than anything to follow Him. In the course of that week, I shall never forget learning how to

---

[1] My soul was regenerated through the speaking of the words in the Authorized Version, the translation I had heard as a child. God spoke to me, thus, in the 'heart language' I knew so well, yet knew not at all: 'For by grace are ye saved through faith; and that not of yourselves: it is the gift of God: Not of works, lest any man should boast' (Eph. 2:8, 9 KJV).

share my faith with another person, and then going out, for the first time, with my friend Charles to present the Gospel to others. I do believe that the Gospel is best presented in a 'lifestyle' way, as a friend, a co-worker, or in a more relational way than I did it that first week. But I can tell that I am certain that the people who received Jesus Christ as Lord that week, to the degree that they were sincere, will be in heaven. I don't think they care whether I was their friend first or their preacher first.

I can still feel the joy of praying with a young woman to receive Jesus Christ, right in the middle of Bourbon Street in New Orleans. I had prayed with my partner, Charles, that God would lead us to someone to share Jesus. At that very moment, this young woman approached us to present the claims of her religion, an Eastern religious sect. We listened and then shared the Gospel of Jesus Christ. Her entire demeanor changed from the aggressive follower of a religion to a human being very aware of her sinful condition and her unmet longings for meaning and purpose. The Gospel produced not only a sorrow for her sin, but a thirst for righteousness and a faith to receive Jesus Christ as Lord. I led her in prayer, and then she, too, prayed with the vocabulary of a child: 'Lord Jesus will you save even me?' For the first time in my life, I was used by God to share His grace with another human being. Actually, it was not the first human being. She was the second.

That first night, after I had realized that I had never truly understood God's grace and that eternal life was a gift by a loving God, not something to be earned or lost, I wanted, more than anyone else, to tell my wife. And I did. New Orleans was about two hours from our home in Prairieville, Louisiana, on Interstate 12. I drove as fast as I could to tell Mae. When I showed up, she was surprised since I was not supposed to be home for that week. I rushed in the door of our home and asked her to join me in the bedroom to tell her something. There I explained the Gospel of Jesus Christ as I had just heard it. As she heard of God's grace and salvation as something God did for us, rather than what we did for God, she said, 'Really?' – and her response was not a response of doubt but of amazement and faith. Together we knelt on the floor of the bathroom, adjoining our bedroom, and committed our lives to this God of grace.

I can testify that life has not been the same since. There was a Mike Milton who lived before that time, and there has been a Mike Milton living since then, but they are not the same. On that night, God gave me a purpose in life: to share His grace with as many people as I could until He called me home. What He put in my heart then has never left me – teach and preach and witness to others about this God-Man, Christ Jesus, His amazing love and grace and power to transform our lives, our relationships, our world. I have let Him down many times, but He has never let me down – not once. He has been good to me. I shiver with chills as I just think about how God came to me in that day.

Something else happened to me that week. Not only did I come to full faith in Jesus Christ as Lord, but I came to see His grace as the scarlet thread that connects the entire Word of God. Someone there, another 'student' at the clinic, who was a medical doctor from Mississippi, gave me a copy of the Westminster Confession of Faith. He told me that this document, unknown to me at the time, was a source of comfort to him since it answered, in a thoroughly biblical manner, the great questions of the faith. I took it and consumed it. I found that, indeed, the questions I had long held were answered, and answered with profound brevity. From understanding that all that we know begins with God's Word (Chapter One of the Confession) to bowing before the simple, untangled biblical facts of His return and the New Heaven and the New Earth (without the complicated Dispensational scheme that had been placed before me by those who, also, could not make sense of it, without 'notes'), I felt that I had 'come home' theologically and biblically. During that one week, I was also introduced to the writings of Francis Shaeffer, and through Shaeffer to

Calvin. Doctrine then took on flesh, and a worldview began to emerge, almost in hours. Truly, I went to Evangelism Explosion one man. I returned another. I have never been the same human being. I was, in every sense of the word, spiritually born again.

If the Lord used Ephesians 2:8, 9 to regenerate my dead soul, He used Romans 8 to heal my wounded spirit; for in that, through Dr. Kennedy's messages, I came to embrace the mysterious truth of God's sovereignty. I shall bless these words until I die, and then I shall bless the Word Himself throughout eternity, by His grace:

'And we know that all things work together for good to them that love God, to them who are the called according to his purpose' (Rom. 8:28 KJV).

Herein was a sacred mystery now revealed to my wandering, hungering soul. Here is the power of heaven in which, as the Puritan Thomas Watson taught, God could take poisonous things, which individually could kill us, and place them in the mortar dish, and with His sovereign pestle, grind them together with the life and death of Jesus and create healing salve. I did not know that I could embrace the very things that sought to destroy me. Miroslav Volf wrote that he could view himself as 'a person who was terrorized by powerful people against whom [he] was helpless and whose intentions [he] could not discern. Or [he] could see [himself] primarily as a person who, after some suffering, has been delivered by God and given a new life, somewhat like the ancient Israelites, who in their sacred writings saw themselves not primarily as those who suffered in Egypt but as those who were delivered by Yahweh.'[2] This is what happened to me. I saw my identity, for the first time, not as hopeless victim in a world of cosmic chance, but an object of divine affection in a plan of sovereign grace. My world, thus, shifted. I did not understand the fullness of His

---

[2] Miroslav Volf, *The End of Memory: Remembering Rightly in a Violent World* (Grand Rapids: Wm. B. Eerdmans Publishing Company, 2006), 26.

sovereignty any more than I understand it fully now, after years of theological inquiry. I simply bowed before this God of sovereign grace, happy to leave my life with Him. Secure in a love that would never let me go, I rose a new man and went home to tell what wonderful things God had done for me.

The first song that I wrote when I returned was about God's sovereignty:

'Of all of the things I've been told,
there's none that more thrills my soul
than knowing that God's in control,
it gives me the strength to go on.
Whether it's good or it's bad;
no reason for me to be sad;
God's given us all that He had,
when He gave up His only Son.'

Refrain:
'He's in control,
He's in control,
tenderly sculpting my soul,
to the image of Christ my King;
He's in control.'

'There was a time when I thought,
life was a chance to be bought,
but I was confused and distraught
by the lies that I'd been told,
So God in His mercy and might,
allowed me to see the Light,
and I know now that it's all alright,
I know who is in control.'

Refrain

'In the darkest night of your soul,
when the storms of life begin to blow,

You can rest your head on this soft pillow,
and you can know…
He's in control,
He's in control,
tenderly crafting your soul
to the image of Christ your King,
He's in control.'[3]

I would later write, in the linear notes of my first musical album, 'He Shall Restore,' these words:

'Of all of the truths I've been told,
there's none that more soothes my soul,
than knowing that God is in control,
it gives me the strength to go on.'

I wrote this song when first I understood how the sovereignty of God was my only hope. My prayer in writing it was and remains to glorify the God of grace and to commend His loving oversight to all who cast their burdens on Him. In Christ, the very thing that seeks to destroy you becomes the thing that brings you life.'

This is my story, this is my song. This is the one sermon of my life: the things that were to be used to destroy me became, in the loving hands of a sovereign Father, the things that led me home.

---

[3] *'He's In Control'* © 2005 by Michael Anthony Milton.

12

Under the Wings of Wisdom

> 'You then, my child, be strengthened by the grace that is in Christ Jesus.' (2 Tim. 2:1).

> 'Oh, what low, despicable thoughts you have of the glorious Immanuel! Lift your eyes from your own bosom, downcast believer – look upon Jesus. It is good to consider your ways, but it is far better to consider Jesus. Oh, believer, consider Jesus. Meditate on these things. Look and look again, until your peace flows like a river' (Robert Murray McCheyne).

My child, I must remind you that wherever you are, whatever condition you are in, if you have breath, there is hope. For Jesus is hope. He is the yes to all of the promises of God. And a disappointing future is not chiseled in stone by the victimization in your past. Fatalism might say so. But Calvinism, so often mistaken for the sad countenance of fatalism, is just the opposite. This is not simply a philosophical system or a religious-political leader, or a stern, didactic textbook religion. But the doctrines of grace are the lively God-centered, Word-saturated faith that are nothing less than the optimistic, forward-looking faith preached by Jesus and by Paul. And this is your hope as it was mine. My son, my daughter, the new life after faith in Jesus Christ is not necessarily a walk in the rose garden, but perhaps a walk to the gallows! As Bonhoeffer said, 'Jesus bids a man, "Come and die!"' That may very well be our lot. But this I must say to you, as one who has journeyed into the far country: hardships in my Father's house cannot compare with the loneliness and desperation of the best of times in the far country. I am like David who said that he has found a place under the altars of the Lord:

> How lovely is your dwelling place, O LORD of hosts! My soul longs, yes, faints for the courts of the LORD; my heart and flesh sing for joy to the living God. Even the sparrow finds a home, and the swallow a nest for herself, where she may lay her young, at your altars, O LORD of hosts, my King and my God (Ps. 84:1-3).

I have spent a spiritual inheritance foolishly in the land of lifelessness. I say that singing 'Blessed Assurance' off-key to the accompaniment of an old, out of tune organ, with country people in Iowa, in a decaying chapel, is to be preferred to the most sophisticated sounds of the world. And so David wrote of singing in the House of the Lord: Blessed are those who dwell in your house, ever singing your praise! *Selah'* (v. 4).

I love the way David says of the redeemed people of God,

> As they go through the Valley of Baca they make it a place of springs; the early rain also covers it with pools. They go from strength to strength; each one appears before God in Zion (vv. 6-7).

Truly, I have learned:

> For a day in your courts is better than a thousand elsewhere. I would rather be a doorkeeper in the house of my God than dwell in the tents of wickedness. For the Lord God is a sun and shield; the Lord bestows favor and honor. No good thing does he withhold from those who walk uprightly. O Lord of hosts, blessed is the one who trusts in you! (Ps. 84:10-12).

This does not, I say again, does not equate with the 'health and wealth Gospel' of some, but it does say that there is a deep-down joy and blessing that follows believers in whatever their condition, however hard or smooth their paths.

One conviction I have from Scripture is that God has a plan for each and every one of us. It is not secret, not mystical, not beyond finding out, not a game of guessing providence, but a plan that, like His very nature in Scripture, unfolds as we follow Him. This is how that path has unfolded in my life.

As I look back at how God saved me and set me on a path of following Him, I am amazed. It seems to me now that He was ordering each and every step of my life to conform to His purposes, which I am only now beginning to understand. All I knew then, and really all I know now, is that I am to follow Him. No sooner had I returned from Evangelism Explosion, than my company, Ashland Chemical Company, promoted me to become a district manager of their operations in the Midwest, in Kansas City. And so we moved to Kansas.

I have written a song about Kansas, used illustrations about Kansas in my sermons, and always refer to Kansas with almost a sense of reverence. Many have wondered, 'why?' Well, God made us to reside in a 'place.' Theologians write about 'holy space' – a place where God does great things in our lives. In the Bible, Abraham's grandson, Jacob, met God at a certain place, and through his meeting with God, Jacob changed the name of the city: 'And he called the name of that place Bethel: but the name of that city was called Luz at the first' (Gen. 28:19 KJV).

I found a place named Kansas, but for me it became the place where God dealt with me. Kansas was the place where God established me in the old Reformed faith, so rich in grace and positive in outlook. There God strengthened my marriage to Mae, showed me in His Word what it was to be a husband and to be a father. God met with me in my hard times as I grieved over being separated from my children. Many hours of weekly prayer, for almost a decade, were made in that place. God settled my Aunt Eva with us there and gave her a better life than she had ever had in rural Louisiana. There God shaped my thinking, even as He bent my will toward His good intentions for me. There I grew to love Jesus. There I came to understand that God would call me to preach the unsearchable riches of Christ I once missed and to declare the name I once blasphemed. That is why, for me, Kansas became 'Bethel.' The Kansas landscape, so wide open, became a living metaphor for the expansive grace of God in Christ. The beauty of her magnificent giant skies reminded me of the beauty of God's incomprehensive love. Even the history of that place, where optimistic pioneers left to settle a new land, to stake a claim for the future, reflected my own story. I, too, was a pioneer following God to where He would lead. For the first time in my life, I felt that I was 'staking a claim' for the future.

This was truly my Bethel.

But my 'Bethel' was also an Antioch. In Acts 13, Antioch was a city where a great church met and worshiped and sought the Lord's will. Paul and Barnabas, along with Mark, were sent out from Antioch to spread the Gospel. But at Antioch they were filled with the Holy Spirit for the work they would be called to do. Olathe, Kansas, specifically Olathe Presbyterian Church (now Hope Presbyterian Church), became our Antioch. The pastor and teacher who grounded me in the Gospel of grace was a man I still call my 'Pastor Bob.'

Robert L. Baxter is my father in the faith. While the late Dr. D. James Kennedy, through his Evangelism Explosion ministry, led me to see God's grace, Pastor Bob taught me how to accept it. Week by week, through expository preaching of the Word of God, the Holy Spirit brought healing to my wounds and nourishment to my soul. Pastor Bob's sermons were so grace-filled, so God-glorifying, so Christ-saturated, and applied with such wisdom and knowledge of the human condition – of *my* condition – that I was literally transformed into a new person yet again. Added to this growth through Bible preaching, Pastor Bob and his wife, Marylu, would invite us to their home after Sunday night services. There we would dine on the rich midwestern fare of Marylu (including her famous cinnamon rolls) and the theological insights of Pastor Bob. Often as we enjoyed the splendid moments at the end of each Lord's Day, he would further apply the expository truths of the particular Scriptures preached that day. Since then, Sunday nights have remained, for me, a beautiful, heavenly time of the week. I associate that time with warmth, rest, friendship, love, beauty of family, glory of God, and, yes, good food!

During those days in Olathe, not only did Pastor Bob and Marylu minister to us, but his son, Mark, and their daughter, Mary, and son-in-law, Kent, became more than friends. I consider them to be family. They, too, welcomed us into their holidays and birthday parties. I will never be able to fully repay them for showing me what family ought to look like. God promised that He would provide family when we had none:

> 'And Peter said, "See, we have left our homes and followed you." And he said to them, "Truly, I say to you, there is no one who has left house or wife or brothers or parents or children, for the sake of the kingdom of God, who will not receive many times more in this time, and in the age to come eternal life"' (Luke 18:28-30).

Through Pastor Bob and his family, Jesus' promise to us was fulfilled completely.

Pastor Bob asked me to teach the adult Sunday school. It was a large class, and I enjoyed preparing lessons from God's Word. I also enjoyed teaching them and expounding upon the lessons to the people. I felt like 'The Flying Scotsman,' Eric Liddell, the great Olympic medal-winning runner who said:

> 'I believe God made me for a purpose, but he also made me fast. And when I run I feel His pleasure.'

So I began to sense that God had made me to preach. And when I preached, I could feel His pleasure.

During this time, I also started an evangelistic outreach into the community and was able to train others to share the Gospel of Christ. One of those, Mark Baxter, Pastor Bob's son, later would take what he learned in those halcyon days, and bring that same message to people all over the world. He remains today a leader of a missions agency in Florida that equips church planters to go to unreached peoples to preach the Gospel. But, for Mark, as well as others, it started with what we called 'screen door evangelism.' Many times our evangelistic teams, who couldn't gain an invitation to enter a home, would share Christ on the front porch through the 'screen door' rather than leave without giving them Jesus. People were saved. Lives were transformed. Jesus Christ was magnified in our midst. My wife also helped me and was involved with evangelistic outreach. Mae would go to the famed Country Club Plaza, an affluent shopping district in Kansas City, and share the Gospel of Jesus Christ on the street corners. Sometimes people would ask which cultic group she was with. She would reply, 'We are from the Presbyterian Church!' That would always shock them! But our church, under Pastor Bob's leadership, was reaching into the community and seeing the Kingdom of God emerging in surprising places.

During this time, I was elected by our congregation to be a ruling elder. I was ordained and installed into the session of the church. I could not believe how God was using a washed-up Methodist lay preacher, a backwoods boy from Louisiana, to help lead a great Bible-preaching congregation in suburban Kansas City.

My Aunt Eva worshiped God with us in those days. She had seen her boy brought by the Holy Spirit from the far country back to the Father's House, now serving Him as an elder in His Kirk. She praised God openly for this miracle. But she would tell me, 'I always knew God would answer my prayers. Even when you were little and life was so hard for you, I knew that God had something special planned for you, Mike. What God starts, God completes.'

I reiterate: The Lord Jesus has a plan for every believer. If God has called you, He will change your dwelling into 'Bethel' – the House of God. For me, that was Kansas. For you, it may be right where you are today. But the important thing for you to know is that God is there and nothing can ever be the same again. When God calls you to Himself, He brings someone into your life to open up His Word to you, to teach you and encourage you in your faith in Christ. Maybe that person is a pastor, a Sunday school teacher, a Bible teacher, a coach, or a neighbor. God raises up His holy servants to equip others. If in the process of leaving this world to follow Him, you lose some things – even relationships – the Master will bring new relationships into your life. This is His promise. I know it to be true from reading His Word, and from my own experience.

My activity in church, later in our presbytery (I was part of the founding of what became the Heartland Presbytery of the Presbyterian Church in America), and in the community was purposefully leading me to conclusions about my life and future. I began to believe, with my wife, that God was calling me into the ministry of the Gospel as a preacher of grace, but I was confused. How could God use someone like me in the Gospel ministry?

13

No Crippled Priests, Only Broken Ministers

> 'I thank him who has given me strength, Christ Jesus our Lord, because he judged me faithful, appointing me to his service, though formerly I was a blasphemer, persecutor, and insolent opponent. But I received mercy because I had acted ignorantly in unbelief, and the grace of our Lord overflowed for me with the faith and love that are in Christ Jesus. The saying is trustworthy and deserving of full acceptance, that Christ Jesus came into the world to save sinners, of whom I am the foremost. But I received mercy for this reason, that in me, as the foremost, Jesus Christ might display his perfect patience as an example to those who were to believe in him for eternal life' (1 Tim. 1:12-16).

> 'Always remember: preach out of your brokenness, and your weakness is God's power!' (The Rev. Robert L. Baxter).

There are times when I think, 'I have known God's call on my life to preach the Gospel ever since I can remember.' I think back through my life, and even in my childhood as I suffered abuse, I knew. Under Aunt Eva's godly guidance, her teaching, times in her lap learning the Scriptures, I knew. I know this sounds unorthodox, but even when I was a prodigal child, I think I knew. I knew that God had placed His hand on me, like Jeremiah, before I was born, and He had ordained me to proclaim the unsearchable riches of Jesus Christ to others. Of course, in God's timetable, I had to experience those riches myself. I had to know of the yearning of the soul for God. I had to personally experience the pain and hellishness of being apart from God. I had to know the joy of coming home to the Father and being accepted because of His love and grace alone. I had to be able to love the Bride of Christ. I had to learn to sing with the hymnist:

> 'I love Thy Kingdom, Lord,
> the House of Thine Abode…'

After a life of abuse and heartache and failure, I came to receive God's gracious gift, to trust in Christ alone for eternal life, and to become His true disciple. I came to follow Him and lead others to Him. I came under the preaching ministry of Pastor Bob and grew to love the warm and winsome understanding of the old Reformed faith. I sought to walk in the 'old paths' and relish them. I followed the Lord through the pain of my past, and the pain of my past became the pathway to earnest prayer. My wife and I had committed our lives to Jesus Christ no matter where that took us. For the time being, we had followed Him in my career as a Fortune 500 manager. My career was soaring in many ways. But I knew. I knew God was calling me.

Later I would come to understand how John Calvin spoke of having both an inward call as well as an outward call. The inward call is that 'still small voice' which checks your spirit, redirects you to God in prayer, gets your attention, arrests you and causes you to look upward. The outward call is the approbation of God's people to the inward call – the practical, the circumstantial, all working together like planets in orbit miraculously aligning so as to not miss the effect of Providence. One friend describes this outward call like a 'parade of Providence' marching through our lives, signaling the arrival of God into our lives. I began to – not know, for again I think I knew in some way all along – but to 'surrender' to God's call to preach His Gospel. During these days, in the late 1980s, I also began to recognize God's outward calling to me. It came through sweet, little old ladies in the back of the Sunday school class who would approach me after I taught.

'Son, have you ever given serious thought to the ministry?'

'Yes, Ma'am, I have.'

'Well, I think you are the kind of man the Church needs. If you were to ever go off to seminary, we would want to help…'

Those kind of encouraging words were frequent. Mae knew this too. She encouraged me in this call and believed that this was where the Lord would lead us. She once told me, when I was selling chemicals, that 'one day you will have something far greater to talk to others about.' My wife always knew.

It is not as though I surrendered immediately. No. I went through my 'Jonah' days. Jonah, of course, when called by God to take the Gospel to the great but wicked city of Nineveh, wanted to go the opposite direction. He bought a one-way ticket to Tarshish. My attempt to run from God caused me to apply to the University of Kansas Law School. When I told my wife, she just looked at me and responded, 'You are running from God.' The application was immediately withdrawn, and I sought an appointment with Pastor Bob.

Here is what I was running from: I had no idea that God could use me. After the mistakes I had made, the sins I had committed, and the sins committed against me, all seemed to add up to a 'no go' for the ministry. During this time, I had read the many opinions about qualifications for the ministry. There seemed to be two great schools of thought. There were those who felt that a man who had been divorced could, possibly, go into the ministry, given the time when that divorce happened (before or after conversion), the time that had elapsed, and the proof of a new 'one woman man' life, as well as 'a long obedience in the same direction' (to use Eugene Peterson's wonderful title from his book on Christian discipleship) in all of the areas mentioned in 1 Timothy 3 and Titus 1.

There were others who simply saw certain sins, certain life events even out of one's control, as disqualifying one from Gospel ministry. I had read about Augustine and his sins and, yet, how God used that broken man to advance His kingdom. I had read about John Newton and his prior life of shame as a profligate sailor and, yet, how God had saved him and used him mightily as a parish minister in the Church of England. Of course, I knew about Peter and his blasphemy and abandonment of Christ at the cross. I knew of Saul's sin of not only persecuting Christians and putting them to death, but his participation in the martyrdom of St. Stephen. I knew also of the marriage problems of John Wesley and how God continued to use that great (and controversial) man. I knew of how God used these men in these ways, but I could not get over a certain passage. It may seem odd to you, but I had to deal with this passage.

> 'And the LORD spoke to Moses, saying, "Speak to Aaron, saying, 'None of your offspring throughout their generations who has a blemish may approach to offer the bread of his God. For no one who has a blemish shall draw near, a man blind or lame, or one who has a mutilated face or a limb too long'"' (Lev. 21:16-18).

I intellectually understood that Old Testament ceremonial law had been fulfilled in Jesus. But this Theocratic law against lame priests seemed to speak to me and condemn me. I was a lame man – lame from my sin and the sins of others. Of course, the priest himself could not help his lameness, and in a sense, my life and the pain of my life were beyond me. But here I was. I seemed to be no different from lame men who were denied the Old Covenant priesthood because of their deformity. My deformity was the deformity of my circumstances. I had a scarlet letter on my forehead – the letter 'D' for 'divorced.' I also felt I had the letter 'A' on my back – 'A' for abused and abandoned. God, I believed, could never use me. Yet I felt 'called.' During those months when I dealt with this issue, I went through the most tormented time in my life. Indeed, it was this pain, this question resulting from my own ill-informed exegesis, which caused a spiritual blockage. That blockage would not allow God's grace to flow and would not allow His call to proceed. This is the real reason I wanted to run. I didn't want to face this pain, this question. I was the crippled lamb unacceptable to God. I was the lame priest unusable by the Lord.

I thank God for two mercies. First, for Edmund Clowney's beautiful book, *Called to the Ministry*.[1] That little book by the esteemed, late theologian, pastor, and seminary president helped to clarify and solidify my sense of inward call. I came to see, with Martin Luther, that though I may be gifted to pursue a variety of other vocations, because I have been gifted to preach, I am in the chains of the Gospel. 'Woe to me if I preach not the Gospel of Christ' (from 1 Cor. 9:16). But the chains of Christ are velvet chains. And in these chains I found my freedom. I put down Dr. Clowney's book and knew that Christ had called me to preach; I felt free to leave all else behind and follow Him. But the real issue remained. And, thus, the second grace of this period of my life was, once again, time with Pastor Bob. I went to him with the 'lame priest' passage from Leviticus. Pastor Bob told me the difference between Old and New Testament law. He showed me how these old signs and shadows foretold and portrayed the perfect High Priest, Jesus the Son of God.

---

[1] Edmund P. Clowney, *Called to the Ministry* (Phillipsburg, NJ, 1964).

He also showed me – indeed, he preached the passage to me personally – how, when we received Jesus Christ, His perfect life is given to us and our sins are laid upon Him on the cross. By faith we become, positionally in Christ, a member of Christ's redeemed people. He stressed that in Christ, I was a new creation:

> 'Therefore, if anyone is in Christ, he is a new creation. The old has passed away; behold, the new has come' (2 Cor. 5:17).

I praise God for the truth of Christ's work of redeeming 'crippled lambs' and 'lame priests:'

> 'Once you were alienated from God and were enemies in your minds because of your evil behavior. But now he has reconciled you by Christ's physical body through death to present you *holy in his sight, without blemish and free from accusation* [my emphasis]' (Col. 1:21-22 NIV).

But there was more to what Pastor Bob taught me than the fact that I was positionally holy before God through Christ. Because God has done this, that power which has liberated me to preach Him to others is the power plant of my ministry. Pastor Bob also told me that far from ignoring the pain of my past, I must now embrace it. My weaknesses, through Christ, would become the very thing that God would use to link my life, as a pattern of God's grace, to the lives of other wounded people. He told me that he, too, believed that God was calling me to preach the Gospel – indeed, was calling me to the unique ministry of Word and Sacrament, as a Minister of the Gospel to pastor the flock of Christ – and that I must always preach out of my brokenness. I left his office with a new love for Jesus. I saw my Savior as the One who not only took my sin, but also became my righteousness. He was my righteousness for the ministry. He was my reputation. He was my credentials. I had no other. That was then. That is also now. I have nothing and I am nothing outside of Jesus Christ. I say with David,

> 'I will extol the Lord at all times; his praise will always be on my lips. My soul will boast in the Lord; *let the afflicted hear and rejoice'* [my joyful emphasis!] (Ps. 34:1, 2 NIV).

Now I understand the personal passion in Paul when he gave his *Raison d'etre:*

> 'I have been crucified with Christ. It is no longer I who live, but Christ who lives in me. And the life I now live in the flesh I live by faith in the Son of God, who loved me and gave himself for me' (Gal. 2:20).

Since that moment I have also relished each and every word of that most pastoral affirmation of faith from the Heidelberg Catechism:

1. Q. What is your only comfort in life and death?
   A. That I am not my own, but belong with body and soul, both in life and in death, to my faithful Saviour Jesus Christ. He has fully paid for all my sins with His precious blood, and has set me free from all the power of the devil. He also preserves me in such a way that without the will of my heavenly Father not a hair can fall from my head; indeed, all things must work together for my salvation. Therefore, by His Holy Spirit He also assures me of eternal life and makes me heartily willing and ready from now on to live for Him.'

I praise God with Paul that Christ has called sinners saved by grace to preach His wonderful good news:

> 'I thank Christ Jesus our Lord, who has given me strength, that he considered me faithful, appointing me to his service. Even though I was once a blasphemer

> and a persecutor and a violent man, I was shown mercy because I acted in ignorance and unbelief. The grace of our Lord was poured out on me abundantly, along with the faith and love that are in Christ Jesus. Here is a trustworthy saying that deserves full acceptance: Christ Jesus came into the world to save sinners – of whom I am the worst. But for that very reason I was shown mercy so that in me, the worst of sinners, Christ Jesus might display his unlimited patience as an example for those who would believe on him and receive eternal life' (1 Tim. 1:12-16 NIV).

It is not given for all to preach the Gospel as an ordained minister, but it is for all of us to show forth God's grace and mercy to others. The very thing that has hurt you most, where you feel most vulnerable, where also Christ has shown you so much grace, this, *this* my dearest one, is your God-given connecting point to other human beings. I believe that our essential humanity transcends all cultures and all races and all generations and times. We are all humans, fallen creatures, wounded and lame people, in need of healing.

I think of what Emil Brunner preached when he said that man has three problems: his past, his present and his future. The problem of our past is that we have sin in our past. But Jesus Christ forgives our sins when we trust in Him. We have a problem in our present, for, as Brunner saw, we have hate. Our relationships are marred by the deep sin within our own hearts. We are unable, in the present, to relate properly to God, or others, or even ourselves. But Jesus Christ heals our present. When we trust in Him, He begins the work of sanctifying us and shaping us, sculpting us into the image of Christ our King. The problem of our future is the problem of judgment. All of us will be summoned to stand before the Lord God Almighty, either through death or the Second Coming of Jesus Christ. What are you going to do? Where will you run? How will you stand before a holy God? What about the lust you had for the woman in the crowd, the hatred you had for the other fellow who got the promotion promised to you, the insensitivity shown to the poor as you passed them by in your expensive sedan, the disdain for the things of God and the fleshly love for entertainment, and the extravagant gifts you gave yourself while withholding money that could have supported the preaching of the Gospel – all of these things and more will condemn you on that day. You truly have a problem in your future. But Christ has taken the punishment for all of those sins on the cross of Calvary. Jesus Christ, the Innocent, became sin so that we who are the real sinners might become the 'righteousness of God.' On that Day, we who have trust in Christ's blood and righteousness and have received Him as the resurrected and living Lord of our lives, will be 'openly acquitted' and 'declared just.' Truly, Jesus is the answer for the problem of our past, our present, and our future.

So, with these glorious truths now embedded in my heart as well as my head, I knew that God had called me and that He could even use crippled lambs and lame priests[2] to spread His Word of grace. How I longed to be prepared for this ministry.

Aunt Eva was near ninety at this time and living at a wonderful retirement home called The Good Samaritan Home. This wonderful establishment is owned by an organization affiliated with the Lutheran Church, and we will always be thankful for it. I used to visit Aunt Eva and ask her how she liked it. This woman who had lived in one place for eighty-seven years would tell me, 'Son, I have never been on a cruise ship, but it must be like The Good Samaritan Home! I just love it here! I am so happy I am now a Kansan!' She was so optimistic, so upbeat, so quick to give

---

[2] Lame priests were not allowed in the Old Testament because the priests pointed to the holiness of God for the people. The 'types and shadows' of the Old Testament found their fulfillment in the perfect One without moral blemish, our Lord Jesus Christ. His perfection, when He is received by faith, enables recovering sinners, and even recovering sinners who are called to preach, to become useful in His kingdom.

glory and honor to God, and thus so content. But I was concerned about moving her. And, quite honestly, I was a bit concerned about leaving my job just then. I had hoped that I could hold on to it and go to seminary at the same time. As I prepared to go to seminary, I began an intense study of the Reformed faith. This study was unabated, day and night – or at least every possible moment I could find in those times. Pastor Bob felt that I could actually pass an examination for licensure. So, in Wichita, Kansas, in August, 1989, I was sustained with unanimous vote of the Heartland Presbytery and licensed to preach the Gospel. That very year I also completed all internship requirements for the ministry, while working full time. Now I only needed seminary – and an undergraduate degree.

I had talked my way into selling chemicals for Dow without a degree and had gone on to work my way up and eventually become a manager for Ashland. But now, in order to go to seminary, I needed to finish the bachelor's degree. Although I had earned two years college from the Defense Language Institute and had taken tests at the University of Kansas that had led me to be within only a few hours of graduating, I decided that I wanted to complete my undergraduate work at a Christian institution. I transferred to MidAmerica Nazarene College (now a University). I was able to complete the degree in Management while working fulltime and completing the ministry internship. I count that experience as a pivotal moment in my 'ministry of preparation' because the faculty at MidAmerica Nazarene College taught me research skills that I would use all the way through seminary and later in postgraduate school in Wales. Indeed, I continue to use the approaches they taught me in my work as a pastor each and every week of my life. I also learned, during those days, how to order my life around Mission and Vision and Values and Strategy. The vision I had in those days was the mission I have now: To so preach, evangelize, and equip others to do so, that on the day when Jesus Christ comes again, there will be a multitude of people caught up to be with the Lord in the air – generations of people who told other people, all resulting from my shepherding a flock, mentoring a student, or preaching a sermon. This is what Paul spoke of when he said:

> 'For what is our hope or joy or crown of boasting before our Lord Jesus at his coming? Is it not you? For you are our glory and joy' (1 Thess. 2:19-20).

My hope and joy and crown of boasting before our Lord at His coming will be the people I shared Christ with and the people I shepherded, under Jesus. That was then, and is now, my vision. My mission is the thing that leads to the vision. For me that is preaching and teaching and leveraging every gift God has given me to be deployed in His service, to realize that vision. For me it means using gifts as a preacher, scholar, writer, singer, songwriter, musician, and pastor, to move toward the vision. My values are the non-negotiable, unchanging truths that guide my life: the truth of the Bible, the centrality of grace to biblical Christianity, the priority and urgency of the Great Commission (to baptize and make disciples of Christ and to teach them to observe whatsoever He commanded) and the Cultural Mandate (to 'subdue' the earth with the knowledge of God and the glory of Jesus Christ in all areas of life, not simply religion), and of equipping others to do the same. My strategy for moving toward the mission and the vision involved, in the late 1980s, transitioning out of the business world and into a ministry of preparation. In 1989 I completed the B.A. from MidAmerica Nazarene College. I would not stop, from that moment on until I finished the Ph.D. from Wales in 1998 – nine years of sustained study to prepare for the Gospel ministry. Such an undertaking was challenging, adventurous, rigorous, and at times, it stretched me and my family to the limit. And I would do it all again. They were some of the greatest years of our lives.

I almost blew it, though. I had tried to continue working and to go to a seminary in Kansas City so that I wouldn't have to move my family. As mentioned, Aunt Eva was near ninety and well settled at The Good Samaritan Home. I had actually received a fully paid scholarship, including books, to attend Central Baptist Seminary in Kansas City, Kansas. I thought this would work out well. But it didn't. I do not know the circumstances at the school today, but at that time, although some of the faculty were wonderful, the school as a whole lacked a commitment to the inerrancy and infallibility of the Holy Scriptures. I believe that this commitment is fundamental to the preparation for the Gospel ministry. If two are not walking together in this area of belief, they will always be apart in other areas as well. I was taking classes at night, working at Ashland in the day, and coming home frustrated because of the liberalism I was encountering. My wife knew it couldn't go on. She began to encourage me to think about leaving to go to seminary. To be honest, the thought frightened me. I was not spiritually mature enough to step out in faith and follow God that far. But God has a way of pushing His little eaglets out of the nest and making them fly.

Two things converged to push me out of my protectionist zone. One was a paper that I got back which was all marked up in red ink. It was a paper I had written for Old Testament class. As I saw the paper and its red lines everywhere, I figured I had really made some serious errors. As it turned out, I had used language in which I called the Bible 'the Holy Scriptures' or simply 'the Scriptures.' My teacher, a female Hebrew instructor, wrote all over the margins that I had written this paper without once clarifying 'which Scriptures,' so that the entire paper was wrong. Well, I approached her in her office, with respect and deference, but with some indignation. She called me in without looking up at me.

I spoke. 'Dr. So and So, I don't understand…' I began. She shook her head, without ever looking up at me, 'There are many sacred texts, Mr. Milton. You need to learn that people of different faith groups have respect for their respective text and they too call them "Scriptures."' Flabbergasted, I responded, still with as much respect as I could muster: 'Doctor, since I was at a Baptist seminary, preparing Christian ministers, and studying the Old Testament of the Bible, I rather assumed that I was safe in thinking we were not caring, at this point, about Hindus or Muslims.' I walked out. I finished my coursework for that semester, turned down a scholarship to continue studying there, and proceeded to make a turn that would cost me a great deal of money. But I had come to see that following God was not about money or convenience or even security. Seminary was not punching a ticket or jumping through a hoop in order to get a sheepskin. Seminary had to be a sort of tithe of the years of your ministry. It had to be a true ministry of preparation where a fledgling pastor could sit under the godly teaching and mentorship of pastor-scholars. A lifetime of ministry demanded the best. The best was not ivy walls or free tuition or proximity. The best was where the vision of my ministry and the mission of my ministry could be given unction.

The other thing that just about cost me my testimony was the wrestling I was doing with God about when to leave my managerial position. I was too frightened, too unfaithful to 'let go' of the safety net. But because I was trying to do too many things, some of my work with the company was suffering. The employees knew that my heart was somewhere else (in the ministry). And my boss knew it too. He flew down to talk to me about my situation. And what happened next in my journey from leaving a career to following a call is unforgettable.

14

Leaving a Career to Follow a Call

'"What do you want me to do, Lord? Are you sure you want to use somebody like me?" Like Jacob at the ford Jabbock, I was caught in a gigantic wrestling match between self-preservation in a secure career and surrender to the unknown and the unpredictable. Perhaps you know who won both fights' (D. James Kennedy).

'Then Amos answered, and said to Amaziah: "I was no prophet, nor was I a son of a prophet, but I was a sheepbreeder and a tender of sycamore fruit. Then the LORD took me as I followed the flock, and the LORD said to me, 'Go, prophesy to My people Israel.' Now therefore hear the Word of the LORD"' (Amos 7:14-16, NKJV).

My wife and I began to pray and seek God's will about where we should be trained for the ministry. We investigated several seminaries where men in our denomination are trained. We visited Reformed Theological Seminary in Jackson, Mississippi (I will never forget the thrill of sitting in a class taught by Dr. Douglas Kelly; my heart and head were lifted together in praise to Christ), and Westminster Theological

Seminary in California (Dr. Edmund Clowney was the man who spoke with us about the school; what a beautiful soul in love with Jesus; I recall that I felt like I had been in the presence of a great saint, which I had), and Covenant Seminary in St. Louis (Bryan Chapell was an adjunct professor back then, but I already knew of his reputation as a great preacher). Each of these institutions offered strong academics and rock solid practical training, and each was being used of God to equip pastors and missionaries for the work of ministry. To say we were impressed with them all is not saying enough. But as we were representing our church at the General Assembly of the Presbyterian Church in America, being held on the campus of Biola University in Los Angeles, we heard about Knox Seminary being founded by Dr. D. James Kennedy and others. The seminary was starting with some of the most esteemed professors in our country, including Dr. George W. Knight III in New Testament, Dr. Laird Harris in Old Testament, Dr. Joseph Hall in Church History, and Dr. Robert L. Reymond in Systematic Theology. Pastoral Theology was being taught by Dr. Kennedy himself, with help from Drs. Dominic Aquila and Bruce Fiol, the late David Winecoff, and a host of others (including my good friend, Dr. John Guest, the noted Episcopalian evangelist, who would later be such an encouragement to me in so many ways).

I will never forget how the seminary was introduced. Dr. Kennedy, who was moderator that year, led a processional of professors to the front of the General Assembly. He announced the founding of the school, which would operate under the session of the Coral Ridge Presbyterian Church and the South Florida Presbytery and, thus, be a PCA seminary, under the authority of the courts of the PCA. In the view of some, it was a controversial way to introduce the seminary, but it sure caught our attention! When Dr. Kennedy spoke of founding a 'new "old Princeton"' with an emphasis on a classical seminary curriculum and on preaching and missions, my heart leaped within me. Though we had no idea how it would work out at the time, we were very impressed with the glorious vision articulated that day. How we finally got there is a story in itself.

It was becoming very obvious to others in my company that my loyalties and first love was not working in the business world. Indeed, I believe that if I had stayed any longer at Ashland Chemical, it would have hurt my testimony as a Christian. When God calls you, it is best to leave all and follow Him. Sometimes that takes a wee bit of reorganizing one's life, but it is possible to tarry too long in doing that – because of a lot of things, but in my case it was because of fear. I trembled under the question, 'How can I go off to seminary, leaving a career that allowed me to overcome/escape the uneducated, poverty-stricken background of my past? And how would I take care of my family as I studied?' I am not proud of that moment, but God used even my fears to glorify Himself.

During this time, as we prayed, I came to understand that unless I was able to completely surrender to God in this area and to go and serve Him in a ministry of preparation at a seminary He chose for me, I could never stand before a congregation and tell them to trust God. I had to trust Him in this. This was my first 'seminary class,' if you will. The courage to follow God came not in rationalizing, but finally in a worship service, sitting under the preaching of Pastor Bob. Pastor Bob was preaching from 1 Samuel on Samuel's hearing God's voice. There came a point in his message – and I cannot remember exactly what was said – when Mae and I turned and looked at each other, out of a reaction to God speaking through Pastor Bob at that moment. In that instant we both knew that we were to go to Knox Seminary. This experience confirms for me the truth that sitting under the preaching of the Word of God is one of the most important keys to growth as a disciple of Jesus Christ. In public worship, God meets with His people, and it is there, through the faithful exposition of the Word of God, that our

Lord deploys His workers, comforts His suffering children, corrects and admonishes His own. For so we read,

> 'For the word of God is living and active, sharper than any two-edged sword, piercing to the division of soul and of spirit, of joints and of marrow, and discerning the thoughts and intentions of the heart' (Heb. 4:12).

And we also read how God does, indeed, use worship as a way to clarify His will and call His servants:

> 'While they were worshiping the Lord and fasting, the Holy Spirit said, "Set apart for me Barnabas and Saul for the work to which I have called them"' (Acts 13:2).

We left church that day knowing that God was calling us to go to Knox Seminary, to be a part of its founding and first students. However, we had no idea how we would get there. That decision came in the late spring. Within a few weeks, one of my superiors in the company flew down from his office in Chicago to be with me. He wanted to know one thing: What was going on with me? I had turned down, by this time, two very large promotions. That was simply not done in our organization at that time. There was an unwritten deal: we will pay you well, but when we call, we expect you to move and go where we need you. I had broken that deal twice. I did so because I knew that I could not, in good faith, uproot my family and move to take a greater position when in fact I had a call of God on my life to preach. I picked him up from the airport and we drove to my office. It was a rather quiet ride. When we arrived and sat down, he just said, 'Mike, what is going on with you?' I had agonized about this very moment the night before. I knew that with one word, my entire career would be over.

But in that agony I once again surrendered to the very real presence of God calling me to preach, and for the first time since His call, I said, 'Yes Lord.' So when my boss asked me what was going on, I simply answered, 'God has called me to preach. I am going to be leaving to go to seminary.' I had no idea what his reaction would be, but this man, this unbelieving man, leaned in, looked me square in the eye, and grinned ear to ear, 'Well, why didn't you tell us before?' I was stunned. I had prepared myself for many possible scenarios, many possible responses he might have, but I never thought I would hear or see this! Then, he said, 'Mike, we have all seen how you have become more and more committed to your church and ... well, to God (that part was hard for him to say since he didn't follow God).' Then he asked, 'Where will you go to seminary?' I responded, 'Well, there are a number of good schools out there, but we believe God wants us to go to a seminary in Fort Lauderdale, Florida.'

He leaned back in his chair, rubbed his chin in deep reflection over my answer and then muttered, 'Mike, let me get back with you tomorrow. Maybe we can help.' I was dumbfounded. God had turned the heart of that man toward me. It was another sign among many signs we had seen and would see to confirm that the Lord wanted us at Knox Seminary. I returned home and told Mae. We rejoiced that night and breathed a sight of relief. We had trusted God. We had walked out of our comfort zone and into God's provision, and God had responded exceedingly abundantly above all that we could ask or think.

The next day my boss did, indeed, call. He told me that the man who first interviewed me to come into the organization was now a regional manager over an area that included South Florida. He would take me as a salesman. Moreover, the company would move us to South Florida. Within days of that conversation, Mae and Amy, our daughter, were packing up our car and heading to Fort Lauderdale. They moved in with my professor, Dr. Robert Reymond and his wife, Shirley. I closed up our house, put up a 'For Rent' sign, cashed in my savings, turned in my keys to the Kansas City office of Ashland Chemical, and left my beloved Kansas City in the rear view mirror. That fall, in 1991, I started Knox

Seminary as a 'middler' student, having completed my first year of seminary, while acting as manager at the chemical company. I would go on, in what were some of the best years of our lives, to complete seminary in three years, while working full-time as a chemical salesman and working part-time as an intern at Coral Ridge Presbyterian Church.

I think it is high time for me to pause and say this: in God's calling, in God's guiding, and in God's directing me to seminary, I began to know God in a new way. Trust gained came through trials endured. If God is calling you to follow Him in some way, I testify to His faithfulness in providing a way and in sustaining you.

Let me say a few words about D. James Kennedy. It was an amazing gift of God that I should intern for the ministry under the man responsible, through Evangelism Explosion, for changing my life for the eternal good. I thoroughly enjoyed my time working under him and studying under him. My family was blessed from sitting under his preaching for our time in seminary. My Aunt Eva loved his preaching and would sit right up front in her wheel chair to hear him. She was in her early nineties at the time. Dr. Kennedy always made it a point to speak with her. My wife interpreted Dr. Kennedy's sermons for the deaf. I was able to assist him in worship and occasionally preached when he was out, particularly in the summer. That he is one of the greatest doctrinal preachers of our time is without doubt. That his work in equipping others to share the Gospel of Jesus Christ through Evangelism Explosion is a model for all pastors is an unassailable truth. His entrepreneurial bent, which was used of God to establish Westminster Academy, Knox Seminary, the Center for Reclaiming America, and so many other ministries, will be remembered as a blessing to our generation.

But, for me, the greatest thing I gained from my time with Jim Kennedy was his optimism for the growing kingdom of God. D. James Kennedy believed that preaching could change the world as we know it. He believed that the Gospel has a power to transform men and their culture and their institutions for the glory of God and the good of mankind. That vision of life I now carry with me every day. His Gospel outlook has become mine. I thank God for this father in the faith, and I shall always bless God for the time I had under his ministry.

I would also say that one of the high honors of my life was learning Greek from George W. Knight III, studying Hebrew with Dr. Laird Harris, church history with Dr. Joe Hall, and sitting under the teaching of systematic theology from Dr. Robert L. Reymond. I often would say that the famous Scottish Preacher of the early nineteenth Century Robert Murray McCheyne had his Cunningham, Bannerman, and Buchanan at the New College of Edinburgh, but I had my Knight, Hall, and Reymond! I was privileged to have been in the first graduating class of Knox Seminary and to have been the first recipient of the Preaching Prize and the Prize in Systematic Theology. The gracious bestowment of these honors worked, I pray, not to pride, but to encouragement in the Gospel ministry.

It was during this time that the theology of the Reformers, and particularly the Puritans, arrested my attention in a new way. I felt that I needed more study in some area of the Puritans and this led to my decision to study for the Doctor of Philosophy degree. I remember corresponding with Ligon Duncan, now Senior Pastor of First Presbyterian Church, Jackson, Mississippi, who was at the time, at Edinburgh. Our correspondence helped me to direct my thoughts in this area. I wanted to preach, and believed God wanted me to plant a church and a school, but I desired to continue my studies. I needed a program that was first class, which had faculty interested enough in Puritan studies to oversee a project, but one which would allow me to study through a part-time arrangement. This led me to the Evangelical Theological College of Wales (now the Welsh Evangelical School of Theology or WEST), and, through them, to the University of Wales at Lampeter. Though there are several colleges in Britain that today validate their degrees through Wales, at that time only the Evangelical College did so. The University of Wales, however, required me to appear before their Postgraduate committee chairman and to submit a prospectus for study.

I shall not soon forget a telephone call that came to me one morning as I was in my study in Overland Park, Kansas. It was Dr. D. P. Davies from the University of Wales indicating that they would, indeed, admit me to the program through Evangelical College. I was elated. I had known for some time that God desired that I continue in education. I knew that sometime, somehow He wanted to use me to train others in the Gospel ministry. The Faculty of the University of Wales placed me under the supervision of Canon William Price, an Anglican priest and Professor of History at the University, and Dr. Noel Gibbard, at the Evangelical College, Bryntirion House, Wales. Canon Price would not be considered an evangelical by most, but he was a kind man, and I think a committed minister of Christ. Dr. Gibbard, now retired from teaching, is a warm, involved teacher who guided me through the research and helped me prepare for the final examinations in his home in Cardiff over a fine lunch. I will not soon forget his 'mock trial' and his pressing questions that left me feeling that I had done the research yet he seemed to know the subject better than I!

For five years, then, I conducted research in historical theology. I did so by flying back and forth across 'the Pond' (the Atlantic Ocean!), several times a year at the beginning and about once per year after that. During my extended time in Wales, I would stay in a borrowed bungalow in an idyllic little Welsh village called Ilston. How beautiful are my memories of autumn weeks spent in Ilston, of being awakened by the gurgling brook, the Willy Nilly, and the bleating of the sheep just outside my door. The chilly Welsh air came through openings under the door and I would linger for a bit under the thick quilts. My wife enjoyed the experience of getting the old style bottles of milk delivered right to our doorstep. And we all enjoyed the thick, creamy Welsh milk each morning. I still prefer Welsh butter to all of the butter products on earth! I got to stay in that wonderful place by arrangement with a pastor in Gorseinon, on the Gower, just outside of Swansea. The 'deal' was, that while there, I would preach on Sundays, and I could stay at his bungalow for free. I always felt that I got the better end of things. While there, I would venture out from our little place in Ilston and conduct research at the National Library of Wales in Aberystwyth. I have spent numerous days and nights in that enchanting seacoast village. It might seem like drudgery to some to hear that I spent days upon days pouring over seventeenth century Puritan sermons, diaries, and Civil War tracts, but to me it was not only intellectually stimulating but spiritually invigorating. To see the mighty works of God channeled through the stories of real people with real problems just like mine created a thirst for God in my soul.

From the National Library of Wales, I would often take research trips to Dr. William's Library in London, to Dartford in Kent, and to the breathtaking Radnor Forest area on the border of England and Wales. The research component of my work finally came to its necessary conclusion. Through the help of my professors, Canon Price and Dr. Gibbard, I completed my dissertation in 1997 and defended it in 1998 before the faculty of the University of Wales. My title was 'The Application of the Theology of the Welsh Puritan, Vavasor Powell (1617–1670).' I will never forget three things about that time: One, I will not soon forget how I felt as I went through the oral examinations and went out into the lobby to wait on the 'verdict.' I could be granted a M. Phil., be asked to rewrite, or be approved for the degree. A secretary was there and took pity on me and we prayed, not for acceptance, but for God's will. Secondly, I will not forget how I walked back into the room where I had been examined, and the examination board of internal and external examiners all stood to attention. The Moderator announced, 'Congratulations ... Dr. Milton ...' and they applauded. How did I feel? Well, I felt that God had once more shown me, a filthy sinner saved by grace and a poor boy from the backwoods of Louisiana, that if He could make a donkey talk in the Bible, He could put initials behind my name!

But the third thing I recall was how I felt an absolute compulsion to make a beeline for Kiddiminster. Why there? Because it was there that Richard Baxter had been pastor. And here was a man who used his scholarship to build up the church. He used every means given him to enrich the souls of His flock with the gifts and experiences God had given him. There was a rose blooming at the foot of his statue, in front of the parish church where he was pastor. I picked one of the blooms and put it inside the dissertation I held in my hand. That faded, crumbling rose petal remains today as a reminder:

> 'Everyone to whom much was given, of him much will be required, and from him to whom they entrusted much, they will demand the more' (Luke 12:48b).

During this time, 1993–1997, by God's grace and through God being pleased to use crooked sticks to make a straight path, I founded and was the first pastor of Redeemer Presbyterian Church in Overland Park, Kansas. I had turned down a position at Coral Ridge Presbyterian Church as Minister of Evangelism. I was greatly honored by the call to Coral Ridge, but believed that I was called to preach the Gospel and to focus on that during this early season of ministry. And, of course, there was already a preacher at Coral Ridge! So, out of a love for the place where God brought me almost a decade before and believing that the Lord wanted me to minister the Gospel in our own nation, I set out, with Mae, Aunt Eva, our daughter, and a bad back, for Overland Park. When we got there, we lived in a borrowed room, for we couldn't get into our own home. The rental agent had mistakenly rented our home out for another year to the folks already living there.

For about a month, I not only planned and worked to gather a seed fellowship for Redeemer, I agonized over our housing situation. The matter was finally resolved, and we were able to move back home. In the meantime, I had gathered about twelve people, including us. I was already licensed but needed to be ordained. I had completed my ordination examinations earlier that year, so on July 16, 1993, I was ordained as an Evangelist in the Heartland Presbytery of the Presbyterian Church in America. I have never forgotten that my first love is evangelism, even as a pastor. I pray that wherever and however God uses me in the future, I will be used in some way to equip others who will equip others to make known the Good News of Jesus Christ! That summer of 1993, I invited some people to our ordination at a 'borrowed' church and twelve of them joined us in a rental apartment in Overland Park. I preached from 1 Thessalonians 1, and the church was on its way.

That night, though there were only a few of us, I went through an Order of Worship, and I was so happy to be leading worship and preaching in my own congregation, even if we were a small band of people who were not sure if we could grow beyond that number. Well, grow we did. Once Mae and I returned to our home, we moved the growing congregation (about forty souls) into our living room. During that wonderful time, I would go out and greet people, share the Gospel, and then invite the people to our home on Sunday evenings. We grew to about fifty and sometimes sixty people in our home. People were listening from the kitchen, from other rooms, and crowded all over the living room. If you can believe it, I preached – no longer from the high and venerable pulpit of Coral Ridge – but from behind an old console television set draped with a white sheet! Never has such a more secular instrument been better used for sacred purposes! But to me, that living room with those people was where God had placed me. I was never happier in the ministry. People were coming to Christ and others were being built up in the faith.

In November of 1993, we moved out of our home into the Overland Trails Elementary school. There I would preach, in my black pulpit robe, from under a basketball net. Some of the children would come up to me after the service to see if I could dunk a basketball! My wife was so beautiful and gracious. She was a faithful partner then, as now, in the ministry of the Gospel. Together, we worked very hard at seeking to establish the congregation.

Sometimes, though, even pastors can be very discouraged and even disgruntled in the spirit. Such a thing happened to me on our first Easter service. We had made every effort to get the word out about this new congregation forming. A group of us had gone door to door inviting people in the neighborhood to church. We took out ads in the paper and on the radio. I spent time in equipping our core group for this moment. And on that Sunday morning, that beautiful first Easter morning in our church's history, Mae and I showed up and no one was there! Now, we *had* arrived early, but we surely thought that someone else would be there.

Mae began taking out all of the nursery stuff and setting up the child care and the Sunday School rooms. I retrieved the solid oak pulpit from a keeping room and packed it and the Communion Table into place (under the basketball net), pulling a muscle in my back in the process. Still no one there. 'This is deacon's work,' I murmured to myself. I was grumbling under my breath, looking at the clock, and sweating as I walked briskly over to check on Mae. She was still setting up things for Sunday School. I then noticed that her new Easter dress was smudged. I pointed it out to her. She didn't seem to mind and kept working. Well, I just got a bad case of self pity! 'Here I was,' I thought to myself, 'setting things up for these people and where are they? (Actually, the core group who had worked so hard were simply more confident that they as a group would have plenty of time to do all that I was doing by myself and so were exactly on time!). I was packing the pulpit and the Table on my back, and my wife's smudged Easter dress became a metaphor for all of my anger. Here I had spent good money on that Easter dress and she got it dirty doing what? Setting up a nursery in a school gymnasium!

I believe that our church could have grown more had their founding pastor been a more godly, trusting man. But in that moment, like Moses at the rock when he struck the rock out of anger, I believe that God had to come and minister to me. He did it through the agency of a man from our home missions board. The man came to check on our work. He went to church with us, interviewed our people, looked around our town, and spent time in prayer in a spare bedroom in our home. I was, of course, very interested to hear his assessment. It finally came right before I was to bring him to the airport. We were in a little pizza joint in Kansas City, with my wife seated next to me, when he said, 'Mike, I think the greatest hindrance to your church is your attitude. You need more humility. Your church cannot grow greater than your spiritual condition.' Smack! Right in the ... heart. I said nothing. I took him to the airport. On the way home, I complained to my wife about him as I drove. 'How can he say that when I am giving so much! Does he know about how I invested my own money, my own retirement funds in this ministry? No! And who is he to say this to me?'

Well, it took some time, but the Holy Spirit showed me, through that and some other experiences, that this denominational official was exactly right. I went on a prayer retreat, and as God showed me this truth, the truth of my own pride, I could almost hear Him say to my heart, 'Son, if I have you packing pulpits on your aching back for the rest of your life, is preaching the Gospel of My Son not worth every bit of it? Is the honor of your calling itself not honor enough, or do you also need honor from men? You have your credentials as a preacher. Will you now accept your credentials as a slave?' I have slipped into the professional mode of ministry many times, but I have never forgotten that time with Christ Jesus, the One who left His royal robes in heaven to come and live as a man, as a servant, and die the shameful death of a criminal, His precious, sinless flesh stapled to a Roman made tree on a dung hill outside of a city called Holy. Can I not follow Him without grumbling about where He deploys me in the ministry?

> 'Please forgive me, Precious Lord, for my sinfulness in the ministry. Please remind me that it is an honor to speak your name, to minister the Bread and the Cup to the lips of those for whom You died, and to pour covenantal waters over the heads of those you are calling. Please send me back to Calvary when I become haughty in my call.'

The Lord blessed the establishment of Redeemer Presbyterian Church in Overland Park. So many wonderful things happened there in so short a period of time, including John Michael's birth. We had worked with a Roman Catholic agency in South Florida while at seminary, and soon after we moved back to Kansas City, a fine baby was born in Miami Beach, Florida. I received the call to say, 'Your son is here. He has a place card over his bed that says, "Boy Milton." I think you and Mrs Milton had better give him his name and bring him home!' The day I wheeled Mae and John Michael Ellis Milton out of the hospital in South Florida is one of the greatest days in my whole life. He was baptized at Redeemer and our lives felt complete in many ways.

So we learned about ministry at Redeemer. Our son came to us at Redeemer. Our marriage was strengthened in so many ways there. I guess it will always be home.

Today, the church is a thriving congregation, hard at work getting the Gospel out to the ends of the earth. And they are doing so with firm commitment to the Scriptures and the old Reformed Faith. Westminster Academy is now Kindergarten through High School. I believe that W.A. is the finest school of its kind in the Kansas City area. But I am biased. I can never forget the first day of school, when parents of kindergartners and first graders dropped their little ones off at W.A. I was there to receive each child, to pray with them, and to look the parents in the eye and try to assure them that the dream was coming true. I weep as I write. For I shall never forget those sacred days of teaching the children in our little chapel. And I will never get over the wonderful core group who believed, and, yes, who worked, who worked harder than I worked, to see a beachhead for the Gospel established in that community. I pray God will bless and use that school for generations to come, until Jesus comes again.

I was preaching through the Book of Revelation when Aunt Eva died. The week before, my wife, and John Michael, (just two and a half years old, and seated in Eva's lap in her wheel chair) were enjoying a nice day in the courtyard of the Good Samaritan Home, a Lutheran care facility in Olathe, Kansas. The next week Aunt Eva fell ill, and we were told she was dying. I will speak more to the events of the funeral in the next chapter, but let me only say here that the event caused me, briefly, to return to that feeling of being an orphan. In my ministry I have seen this happen as a person loses both parents. My loss felt severe. She had been God's human and loving relief of orphanage earlier in my life. Now she was gone. Life, ministry, everything, grew silent in my mind and heart.

It was during those days that our home missions board began to ask me to consider planting another church. That might seem ill-advised to some, given that I had only been at Redeemer for four years by then, but the needs are great in our nation, and the workers are few. Sometimes we plant churches, and the man remains there for his whole ministry. Those are often vital, strong churches with a strong pastoral leadership. We also plant churches, like Paul did, by deploying and re-deploying a pastor several times, and seeking to build up strong lay leadership, elders and deacons, in the local church. There is more than one way to get the job done. And so, I was being asked to consider another location to plant a new church. But Aunt Eva's death caused me to pause from all of that.

In those days, I was also asked to step in to become an interim administrator at the seminary that had trained me. Thus, in 1997, I announced to our congregation at Redeemer that the Lord had impressed upon me that I was to follow a call to go to Knox Seminary, in order to preach the Gospel, to spread the word about the seminary around the country, and in so doing, to recruit students. The day I made this announcement was one of the hardest days in my life. I loved Kansas. I had dreamed of planting this church and school. But maybe because of that, the Lord was about to teach me that He is the Lord of the Church. Perhaps whereas some men can found and pastor the same church for their entire careers, I could not. Perhaps for me it would become idolatry. So the Lord removed me from my adopted homeland and my dream for Overland Park. It would remain for our local leaders to finish the dream, and leaders after them, until Jesus comes again.

Dr. Cortez Cooper had been president of Knox Seminary, but had left to lead the PCA's home missions board, Mission to North America. As I stepped into this new role, I enjoyed my work at the school greatly. I was blessed to teach pastoral theology there and as such taught Reformed Liturgics, Preaching, and Spiritual Formation for Pastors. I also helped to revise the curriculum in order to place greater emphasis on preaching. I enjoyed my own preaching ministry, though it took me from home often. There were overtures made to me to become president of the seminary. Indeed, one of those came from Dr. Kennedy. But during my year and a half at the school, I believed that I needed more time in pastoral work before teaching or leading a school. I believed that at sometime in my future I would again invest my hours and days in the equipping of pastors and missionaries and other Gospel workers to fulfill the Great Commission, but I was not ready. I shared this with Dr. Kennedy and he reluctantly and graciously released me to find out how God would accomplish His will in my life. I learned from Dr. Kennedy something more: I learned to trust God in others' lives as I had to trust

Him in mine. Dr. Kennedy modeled for me how to 'let God' be as original in others' lives as He has been in mine.

Hindsight is not only 20/20 as they say, it can be anesthetized. Distance can cause us to list off the events of our lives with little reflection on how those events actually unfolded. In my case, I moved from Redeemer to Knox and then on to another ministry assignment with characteristic halting steps. Indeed, I found that as I ministered, I was still grieving Aunt Eva's death. I was still grieving the loss of a dream in Kansas. I was still grieving over my own wounds. And I was still learning how to minister out of brokenness rather than strength, or at least a feigned strength. I also needed to learn how to discern God's calling. In short, I was still being formed, not just as a minister, but as a believer.

After some stutter starts and missteps, I accepted a call to plant a new congregation in a residential area south of Savannah, Georgia. We moved to Skidaway Island and planted Kirk O' the Isles. The church was funded, as was our previous labor, Redeemer Presbyterian Church, by the Independent Presbyterian Church, Savannah. The minister there, The Reverend Terry Johnson, was a friend of mine. He had believed in our dream of a church and school in Overland Park, Kansas. And now he had a dream and came to me. He believed that there was a need for a new church in the Skidaway Island community. Thus with prayer to God about how we ought to proceed, we turned down other calls to answer this one. We had been living in Kansas, commuting to Knox in South Florida and flying and driving around the nation getting the word out about the seminary, so now we finally had to move from Kansas to Georgia. Those years, from 1998 until 2001, were good years. I have never felt more freedom in preaching, in witnessing, and in counseling. Many people began to come to me for counseling. It was, I think, during this time of planting Kirk O' the Isles that I began to see how God truly would use my brokenness, if I would but open my heart to Him to do so. Many people prayed to receive Jesus Christ as Lord and

Savior. A strong core group emerged, and within the first six months a new congregation was formed, with elders and deacons ordained. Pastor Bob preached the service and Dr. Roy Taylor, Stated Clerk of our national church, led in prayers and gave a greeting from the Presbyterian Church in America. On that first Sunday, our congregation also presented Dr. Taylor with gifts for all of the agencies of our denomination. The vision of having a church that would be a resource and sending congregation from this affluent area of Savannah, Georgia, was now underway.

In 1999, as I was involved in the planting work at Kirk O' the Isles, we returned to Overland Park, Kansas, and Redeemer Church to preach a 'Founder's Day' message. During that visit, a distinguished older couple came to me as I was receiving people after the message. The gentleman introduced himself as being from Chattanooga, Tennessee. I responded with a question as to whether he knew Ben Haden. He told me that he did, indeed, and that he was an elder at First Presbyterian Church of Chattanooga. He was in Overland Park visiting his son and wanted to attend a PCA church and that is how he happened to be there. He informed me that Dr. Haden had retired in 1998 and a search was underway for a pastor.

I gave absolutely no thought to that conversation until December 2001 when I sat at table in the fellowship hall of First Presbyterian Church, Chattanooga. My wife and I were there being honored as the twelfth Senior Pastor in the 163 year history of that church. There, with all of the officers and their wives gathered, Dr. David McCallie, the distinguished gentleman I had met at Redeemer Presbyterian that day, read his letter in which he nominated me as pastor after he returned from that trip. He had heard me and believed that I was to be the next pastor of his church (this meant even more to me when I learned that he is the grandson of the late, great Dr. Thomas Hooke McCallie, the famed pastor of First Presbyterian Church during the War Between the States). As Mae and I heard him read his letter, we held hands and shivered in happy awe and wondrous reverence before the sovereign Lord God who had surely called us there.

The call was a surprise of God. It was not, of course, a surprise *to* God, but His serendipitous gift to us. It was not, in fact, Dr. McCallie's letter that prompted the Pulpit Search Committee to finally agree that I was the one. It was a series of events that led them, after almost three years of searching, to finally receive a letter from my Pastor Bob. Dr. Roy Taylor had told me that he thought I was the man that ought to be the next pastor of that great congregation. I almost fell out of my chair when he said that. But as I told Pastor Bob about the conversation, he believed that he should write the pulpit committee. His letter was apparently so meaningful to the committee that they authorized Muecke Barker, a member of the Tennessee Supreme Court (later Chief Justice of that great body), to contact me. In early September, he did. And within a few weeks he and Scott Brown, an attorney in Chattanooga and an elder in the church, were in our living room. That meeting was followed by other visits and then by a time when the larger committee heard me as I preached a missions conference in Augusta, Georgia. By that time, Mae and I felt in our hearts that if there was an outward call, we would accept. We believed at that point that the Lord was calling us there. Again, it was a total surprise, but on December 9, 2001, the congregation voted to call us, and we accepted the call.

How does one follow a legend who has preached for thirty-two years in the same place? I began my ministry by asking that question to several other ministers who had done it. I credit Harry Reeder, Pastor of Briarwood Presbyterian Church, Birmingham, Alabama, with the wisdom I have found the most practical and honoring to God, at least in our case. 'Honor the past and build for the future.' Well, we set out to do that. The road has often been filled with great challenges. Indeed, I have packed 100-pound iron pipe up and down oil rigs in the swamps of Louisiana; I have managed Fortune 500 organizations' interests in large sections of the nation; I have planted churches and founded a school; I have run a seminary.

But I have never done anything more difficult that being a pastor of an historic, downtown church. That is not to say that it is the hardest thing in the world to do! But the challenge of leading a great congregation like First Presbyterian Church of Chattanooga, Tennessee, with its unsurpassed legacy of faithfulness in missions and in preaching and Christian education, amidst a diverse congregation that includes many of the leaders of our community, our state, and our nation has called for many nights of prayers and tears. If not for the mercy of the Lord and His grace, and the vision I was given at my conversion and during my training under other great ministers of Christ, I cannot imagine how I could do it. But the Lord gives more grace.

When it is all said and done, names change, situations change, but human beings are the same. I am unashamed to say that I believe in what are called 'the ordinary means of grace' for the ministry: Word, Sacrament, and Prayer. I believe as a core conviction that God has given us the way to preach to large congregations and small congregations, the way to plant churches, the way to lead seminaries, the way to train pastors. We teach the Bible. We hold high the sacraments that feed the saints and bring them into the kingdom of God. And we pray and exalt prayer. Ligon Duncan likes to speak about 'Singing the Word, Praying the Word, and Preaching the Word.' I would add 'seeing the Word' in the Sacraments. But the idea is clear: the only way to do ministry is to minister Jesus Christ according to the ways given us in His Word.

Long ago Dr. Jim Baird, former pastor of First Presbyterian Church, Jackson, Mississippi, said to me, 'Son, if you preach to broken-hearted people, you will never lack for a congregation.' I have found that to be absolutely true.

Now where does this leave you, my child? Most likely you are not being called to preach or teach. You will not lead a seminary in training pastors. You will not have to struggle with calls to different churches. But you know struggle. You know pain. You know the longing inside of you to know God, to experience God, and to trust God.

I dedicate this next chapter to you.

15

Locust Fields Redeemed

> 'I will restore to you the years that the swarming locust has eaten, the hopper, the destroyer, and the cutter, my great army, which I sent among you' (Joel 2:25).
>
> 'There is more mercy in Christ than there is sin in me.' (Richard Sibbes, *The Bruised Reed*)

Once, a lady who had lived a very hard life came to me. She came to me to confess Jesus Christ as Savior. Mae and I invited her to join us in our home on Monday evenings. We wanted to help her find her way in the things of discipleship: the Bible, worship, fellowship, witness, and prayer. One night she came to our door and was heaving tears. I thought that maybe she had been in an accident, but she didn't look hurt. As she came in, she fell on my shoulder and wept uncontrollably. She was finally able to speak. She said that God had saved her but that He couldn't ever use her. Her life was too far gone.

It was then that I told her a story. I told her a story about a man I know. I told her about a man whose life, because of his sin and the sins of others and the fallen condition of this world, was like a locust-eaten field. Hardly anything was left that was fit for use. But then God came into this man's life. By the glory of God that is in Jesus Christ, locust fields become arable again. Years lost are regained in the sovereignty of God. Then I told her, 'I am that man.'

The God who saves us is the God who restores us. Redemption is not just an expensive theological word. In Jesus, redemption is reality for the believer. It works out in different ways for different people, but it always, always works. Jesus is our Redeemer, and oh, how those most broken love Him as Redeemer.

I have heard it said that those whom God uses best, He crushes most. My efforts for the Gospel have been small in comparison with much greater women and men of God. But however He measures my usefulness, I can say that He has crushed me. I have been crushed as a little child, crushed as a young person, crushed as a young man, and through many years of my adulthood, I knew the crushing reality of the promise of locust fields redeemed, but not yet brought to fulfillment. The greatest burden I carried was the sense of the loss of children and the pain of having once been called 'Daddy' and not being called that anymore. I wrote these children. I prayed for them. During the many years when I didn't even know where they were, I wrote each of them a birthday card on the occasion of their birthdays and placed it in a special file. I prayed. I prayed daily. My pain was so great that I finally learned that I could not start each day in tears. Therefore, I made a sort of appointment with the Lord. I would go to Him once per week in the evening. I would shut myself in my home office and I would pray and I would cry. Oh, how many prayers went up wet with tears.

I also remember the acute pain in my heart as I saw other children. I recall being in an airport once and seeing a family about to get on a plane. As I looked upon the beauty of family, the love of the parents for their little girl and boy, I was overcome with emotion. Like Joseph in Genesis, I had to run away and hide, in order to weep. I truly was a weeping man. I was saved, but so much was lost.

In those days, Aunt Eva would remind me once again that what God started, He would complete. Philippians 1:6 was etched into my mind and had become my hope:

> 'And I am sure of this, that he who began a good work in you will bring it to completion at the day of Jesus Christ' (Phil. 1:6).

The passage is eschatological in nature. The promise, I realized, might not be accomplished fully in this life. In that sense, I began to grow to love the coming of Christ. I remembered a beautiful little deaf girl in my lap signing to me, 'I can't wait for Jesus to come – then I will be able to hear!' Now, I too, sought to understand the mystery of those who are 'hastening the coming of the day of God' (2 Pet. 3:12) out of their soul-wrenching cry for justice and healing.

Yet Jesus has said that even in this life, His disciples are blessed for what they have lost. I write now, dear friend, to tell you how God restored the years the locusts ate in my life.

The very woman who sought to abort me, my biological mother, became a way that God showed me His redeeming grace. One day, before we left to go to seminary but after I was involved as a licensed minister at the Olathe Presbyterian Church, Olathe, Kansas, I received a surprising telephone call. The call came from a relative of this woman, Marina. He told me that she was dying of cancer. She had lived a hard life. She had suffered from schizophrenia and other mental illnesses. She was poor, but in her final days, going in and out of a coma, she was calling for 'Michael Milton, the preacher.' Mae and I decided that though I didn't know her, didn't know her family, it would be honoring to the Lord for me to fly down to New Orleans to see her. I did. I prayed about what to do, and the Lord directed me to simply read from Romans 8. I flew from Kansas City to New Orleans and drove to the hospital in Mandeville, Louisiana. I went to the information desk, found her room, and made my way there. I can guarantee you that I was praying every step of the way. I walked into the room and there she lay. She was, in fact, in a coma. She was not responding. I walked over to her bed and looked at her. She showed the pain of a lifetime. I do not remember feelings of regret, which I wondered if I might have. I had no sense of bitterness or confusion or questions. She was a human being who had made decisions. She was a sinner who needed to be saved by grace. She did nothing that I was not capable of doing. My thoughts in these areas took only a few moments. I raised my Bible to where I could see it. I turned to Romans 8. I began to read,

> 'There is therefore now no condemnation to them which are in Christ Jesus, who walk not after the flesh, but after the Spirit. For the law of the Spirit of life in Christ Jesus hath made me free from the law of sin and death. For what the law could not do, in that it was weak through the flesh, God sending his own Son in the likeness of sinful flesh, and for sin, condemned sin in the flesh…' (Rom. 8:1-3 KJV).

I read the entire chapter. Then I prayed for her soul. I prayed for mercy in her suffering. I lifted my head, turned and walked out, assuming that the one I had remembered in such pain and confusion as a child, I would see no more. I left the hotel and began my journey back home to Kansas. About one month later, again at dinner, another call came. She had died. But before she died, she came to. When she did, her son, a believer – she had eight other children – had prayed with her to receive Christ. As she did, she asked if they could contact me. She wanted me to conduct her funeral service. And she said something else before succumbing again to the sleep of the disease. 'Michael was here. I heard. He read from the Bible ... Romans ...' Of course I agreed to do the service. She was to be buried in Tylertown, Mississippi, which is where I learned she was from. I figured out that this was likely the place where she had taken me when she had 'kidnapped' me when I was a child. It was no doubt in that place where I remember the old wrinkled Indian face, the old wooden plank floor, and the sense of utter fear. I would go there again but to bury this woman, this sinner saved by grace in her last moments, this mother.

Before I left, I went to pray with Aunt Eva. She spoke few words. She disapproved, but her emotions stifled anything else than 'be careful.' I flew, this time, to Jackson, Mississippi, rented a car, and drove down to the piney woods of South Mississippi. Within a few hours, I was standing in a pulpit, with Marina's coffin before me. I preached the Gospel of grace and invited those who didn't know that grace to receive Jesus Christ. I told them that there was no better place or time to do so. I returned to Jackson and got a hotel room. The next morning was Sunday. I worshipped at First Presbyterian Church, Jackson. The venerable Dr. James Baird was preaching. I cannot remember his text or his title. But I remember that as he spoke forth the Word of the Lord, it became balm for my soul. I was not unhappy. I was not depressed. I was stunned by the unbelievable redeeming grace of Jesus Christ. I still am.

The joy of my life is my son, John Michael. After nine years of marriage, and many tears shed over loss, and many prayers made to have a child, the Lord Jesus blessed us with our boy. He was born in Miami Beach, just as we had left South Florida to begin church planting. I shall never forget the call that said, 'Reverend Milton, it is a boy. Your son is here. There is a sign on his bed in the nursery that says, "Boy Milton." I think you'd better come!' Mae had been visiting in Louisiana and I called her and told her, 'Our boy is born!' I met Mae at the airport as she was flying in. She never went back home. I had packed her bag (with nothing that she could wear, as she now reminds me) and we flew down immediately and went to the hospital. We were tripping over ourselves as we went into the nursery. No sooner had we walked in than a smiling nurse holding a baby with a 'sock' on his little head ambled toward us.

'Reverend and Mrs. Milton?' 'Yes,' we said with a nod. 'This is your son. What's his name?' His name is John Michael Ellis Milton. They put my wife in a wheelchair, placed John Michael in her arms, and after some insurance matters were attended to, we were gone.

John Michael's first night was spent at Dr. Reymond's home in Fort Lauderdale. They were so wonderful to us, showing us the love of Christ during what could have been a stressful time. We love them so. We stayed for seven days. During that time we drove up to see Mae's mother, who lived, at that time, in Melbourne, Florida. We returned to Dr. Reymond's home and on the next day, the first Lord's Day in my son's life, we went as a family to Coral Ridge Presbyterian Church. Dr. Kennedy greeted us and held John Michael. Many other close friends surrounded us that day. I was overwhelmed. Saved through Evangelism Explosion, brought into the Reformed faith by Dr. Kennedy, trained for the Gospel ministry under his tutelage, I now, with our son, sat in the sanctuary of Coral Ridge as Dr. Kennedy preached. What grace. What redemption. We returned home and two Sundays later I baptized my son John (after the Gospel of John and after John Calvin and my Uncle John) Michael (after me) Ellis (after my father). I baptized him in the church we were planting. We dedicated this child to Christ and to His work. He has and continues to bring unbelievable joy to our lives. God redeemed the locust fields.

But what of the others? In September, 1997, my Aunt Eva, at age ninety-seven, fell ill. Congestive heart failure set in. We were told that she was now in that last downward cycle of life that leads to the end of life. We were stunned, because just a week earlier she had held John Michael in her arms as we pushed them around in her wheelchair. But now she lay dying. On a day I shall never forget, Aunt Eva, on her death bed, reached for me, pulled me down to where she could speak to me and told me, 'I love you ... keep up the good work you are doing.' And then she said, 'You will see the children again.' She looked at Mae with a loving look and asked her, 'Where is the baby? Where is John Michael?' Mae lifted him for her to see. She then lifted her hands and blessed us. She was raised half way up in her bed. At her blessing, she fell back down flat on her back. As she did, she started praising God. 'Praise the Lord! Praise the Lord! Praise the Lord!' I called for her, in my grief, not wanting her to go just yet. But having given us her blessing, she had now turned her total attention to the Lord she had served all of her days. She would not be diverted from her worship of Christ. I was preaching through the Book of Revelation during those days. As I contemplated and sought to communicate the glorious truths of heaven to the flock at Redeemer Presbyterian in Overland Park, Kansas, I felt that it was all so much more real to me. Aunt Eva slipped into the arms of Jesus Christ as the Kansas fields were being harvested. I had been preaching from this text:

> 'Then I saw a new heaven and a new earth, for the first heaven and the first earth had passed away, and the sea was no more. And I saw the holy city, new Jerusalem, coming down out of heaven from God, prepared as a bride adorned for her husband. And I heard a loud voice from the throne saying, "Behold, the dwelling place of God is with man. He will dwell with them, and they will be his people, and God himself will be with them as their God. He will wipe away every tear from their eyes, and death shall be no more, neither shall there be mourning nor crying nor pain anymore, for the former things have passed away." And he who was seated on the throne said, "Behold, I am making all things new." Also he said, "Write this down, for these words are trustworthy and true"' (Rev. 21:1-5).

We held a funeral service in Olathe, Kansas, where I preached the service. Kansas had become her home and she loved it there. But she had desired to be buried next to her husband's body at the cemetery at Amite Baptist Church in Watson, Louisiana. We flew her remains to Louisiana, to the old home place, the old faces and names that I had remembered from my childhood. There I was to conduct her service again, but this time Reverend Woody Markert of Plains Presbyterian Church of Zachary, Louisiana, would do the preaching.

I was in the back of the chapel, putting on my pulpit robe, with Mae helping me, when it happened. Aunt Eva had told me that God would answer my prayers about the little ones I had not seen for over a decade. And her prayerful confidence was fulfilled on that day. An older man came up to me and said, 'You don't remember me do you?' I actually did recognize his face, one of the faces of my childhood, a dream like place from long ago. 'Yes Sir, I do remember you.' He smiled, then looked me right in the eye and spoke, 'Son, I know where those children are.' I grabbed my wife for support. I couldn't believe it. And it was happening right as I was about to go out and lead in worship at Aunt Eva's funeral. 'Thank you,' I said. He told me how to contact them and then he left. I never saw him again. Mae and I embraced. I wept and shook with awe. But it was time to start the service. Within only a few months, after some letters, Mae, John Michael, and I flew to Washington, D.C. Mae, who had gone to college to learn sign language in anticipation of this very day, stood by with John Michael and snapped a picture of a joyful, tearful reunion. We returned two more times, snapped two more amazing pictures. The prayers of Aunt Eva, of Pastor Bob, of our family, had been answered. And those prayers are still being answered. But I don't hear locusts any more.

God saves us. God transforms us. And God, in Christ, redeems. He is doing so now and will do so until at length, He comes again, and brings in a new heaven and a new earth. And here is what I want to say to you: I don't have easy, pat answers for your problems. But I know this: our desperation is the starting point for prayer and the thing that God uses to bring about His kingdom in our lives. 'Humble yourselves under the mighty hand of God and He will exalt you in due time.' Peter said that. Peter knew.

Peter knew first hand. For the man who had blasphemed and deserted his Friend, who had seen the empty tomb but couldn't rejoice because of an empty, unforgiven heart, had heard the words, 'Feed my sheep.' Peter understood that in his brokenness, not in his boastfulness, God was honored and he was used. This is the way of the Lord.

'Always preach out of your brokenness,' Pastor Bob told me. Now I understand, 'Always *live* out of your brokenness.' For there is strength, divine strength, in trusting in Christ and not in yourself. And where locusts once devoured your fields, Christ now cultivates them anew. The very thing which was used to destroy you has become the thing that saves you. 'This is my story, this is my song, praising my Savior all the day long.'

16

A Humble Appeal to Hurting Hearts

> 'And I am sure of this, that he who began a good work in you will bring it to completion at the day of Jesus Christ.' (Phil. 1:6).
>
> 'Live near to God, and so all things will appear to you little in comparison with eternal realities' (Robert Murray McCheyne).

I have told you my story. And now maybe you have a better understanding of why I say, 'My only identity is in Jesus Christ.' I have no other philosophy for living, and no other assurance in dying. I have no other confidence for today, and no other hope for tomorrow.

'So,' you may say, 'I have this fellow pegged. He is a successful clergyman telling his story. He was once a loser, and now exudes confidence and success. He lost a lot, but now has it all together.'

I am afraid, child, that you do not have me pegged at all if you believe that. The only thing that, perhaps, separates you from me is one word: home. I am not there, but my Father has welcomed me home and I have never known such grace as when I received his welcome. It was not my decision. It was and is His welcome that is the moment of grace, the moment of conversion, if you will.

I will tell you of the wonders of this new life and I will tell you of the challenge.

Here is the wonder. Take today, for instance. I read devotions to our family. We are in the Psalms right now. Tonight was Psalm 24. 'Who is this King of glory?' How we know the answer to that question. The King of glory is our Lord Jesus, the Redeemer. After reading it and teaching from it, we sang, 'Praise Him, Praise Him, Jesus our blessed Redeemer…' and we smiled as we sang. I could hear my son's voice in harmony with my wife's voice and that of my own. There was a grace in that, not just a musical milestone, but a real power at work. Lives singing in harmony to the music of hymnody is precious. But it is only the outward playing. There is a deeper, inward song. This is the song of grace. It is the music of heaven in redeemed sinners. But I continue.

We prayed. After prayer, we went through the Shorter Catechism, a teaching device our own church uses to help us grow in the truths of the Bible. We had not studied from it in a while. My son, who is now twelve, needs to move beyond the classical 'grammar' of the subject and interact more with the issues at hand in the subject. So tonight we talked about God, His being, and His work of salvation. We talked about the role relationship of the Persons of the Godhead: Father, Son and Holy Spirit. I thanked God for this moment. Then, and you may not find this too holy for a preacher to do, we watched a great, old Sherlock Holmes movie – 'The House of Fear' with Basil Rathbone and Nigel Bruce. That may not seem very religious to you, and if one thinks of life in neat, but separate compartments, I guess it isn't really very religious. But the wonder of that moment is that, from this vantage point, I can now taste joy in the mundane things of life. Indeed, I rather relish this new wonder as much as I do any other. Like a smoker who quits and then discovers the taste of strawberries, or rain on your tongue in the spring, I can now taste the simple joys of life. The Gospel opens up our senses to enjoy life, and, in a word, to be happy. I know people who have been to Mass at St. Peters in Rome, to tent revival meetings in Kentucky, and to Matins at St. Paul's who are still most unhappy. I will take joy and peace and Basil Rathbone over religious feelings with no lasting value any day of the week. After the movie, we talked about everything and nothing, and my wife put my son to bed. Before they went upstairs, they kissed me.

Tomorrow, Lord willing, I will preach a message to saints gathered for a funeral. I will have a staff meeting with ministers and directors of our church, as we plan for worship this coming Lord's Day. Then I will leave to go out of town to be with a family undergoing a kidney transplant. I will be there to pray with them and bring the comfort of Jesus and His Word to them. I am also working as a board member with Knox Seminary and chairing a committee to think about our future as a seminary. I am a United States Army Reserve chaplain and am thinking about my ministry with our troops coming up this month. I could just as easily be going through any other man's day, but this is my day. This is God's wonder in my life. These are the tiny and the gigantic miracles, the personal and the cosmic rearranging of my own world. There are others who are carpenters and lawyers and homemakers and bankers and plumbers who have their stories, their stories of how God's story arrested them and transformed them and gave them new stories.

This is the wonder. This is the wonder of the Gospel of the God-Man, Jesus: prodigals preaching Jesus to people who are truly better men and women than they are; broken families laughing though the distance still divides them; arms lifted high and giving benedictions through the scar tissue of past sins; living testimonies of new life who still weep at the funerals of loved ones, just like everyone else; struggling saints listening for God's voice against the cacophony of voices screaming 'this can't be so' in their own minds; crippled old men in nursing homes called the 'sons of God' sipping wine from a chalice called 'Christ's blood' and chewing wafers called 'the Body of Christ' and spilling their salvation all over themselves as they do; God in a feed trough when a special Star crosses the nexus between timelessness and time in a forgotten town in an occupied country; 'Immensity in Thy dear womb,' adopted by a man named Joseph and living under the authority of a pagan government; God on a cross; God dead by the hands, in one sense, of those He created; God dead and God alive; God living in me, in you. God living in this very human, very divine organism He calls His Bridge, the Church.

And here is the challenge: accepting the gift of wonder for yourself.

'I am not good enough.' 'I tried doing the religious thing, it didn't work for me.' 'My mother did this and it drove me nuts.' 'I can't believe, too much has happened.' 'I want to believe, but…' I know. Do you hear me? I know. I have been there. But the wonder is nothing like the trip home. The wonder is that He is always there. He has always been there. The wonder is that God takes the first step. He may have done that through this book. He may be doing that in your soul right now. The wonder is, in a word, God with us, Emmanuel: a wonder that is for all, for any who will receive the welcome home.

I once preached a sermon entitled, 'What God Starts, God Completes.' The title comes from the truth of a particular, wonder-filled passage that God wants you to know:

> And I am sure of this, that he who began a good work in you will bring it to completion at the day of Jesus Christ (Phil. 1:6).

This teaches us that the greatest work in our lives is not the one we try to ignite, but the one He makes out of nothing, for Paul says, 'He who began a good work.' And it says that He does this good work, this beautiful, creative work of new life, in 'you,' that is, in ordinary people like you and me. It also says, and I know of no other wonder greater than this in the believer's life, that God will bring to completion what He has started.

What does all of this mean? How does Philippians 1:6 work in your life?

There was once a lumberjack who took his little son with him into the woods for the day. While there, a great storm came up, and the creeks in the woods began to flood. The two were practically trapped between the woods and their home by a swift-moving creek that was rising by the minute. At the bank of that creek the dad took his little son into his arms and held him tightly. The little boy, out of sheer exhaustion, fell asleep on his father's shoulder.

The next thing the boy knew, he was awakened to see the morning sun flooding through the curtains in his room. He was in his own bed, clean, dry, and safe. His father was leaning on the doorway with a mug of coffee in his hand. He was giving the boy his usual first smile of the day.

You see, God is like that. When, in the storms of life, it seems that the problems of life begin to rise so fast that we could never get home again, we can rest in our all-powerful father. God will carry us through the worst of storms all the way home. He *is* carrying us now, even if we do not want to admit it.

God began the work in my life, and in the midst of the storms, I finally learned to trust in His sovereign power.

You can do that, too; right now. And you will one day wake up to see that He brought you safely all the way home.

God's promises bring abundant life here and now and eternal life with Him when we die.

I invite you who have never seen this wonder to turn from the empty idols of this age, to repent of a religious journey that seeks to get you home without God's love in Jesus, and to commit your life to Jesus Christ alone for eternal life. In love, and as a fellow believer often blinded by the dullness of a boastful, empty pride or enticed by a shiny new gimmick for knowing God, I encourage you to re-commit to the wonder of a Father's love, a Son's sacrifice, and the Spirit's unbounded power. We can do that through that most ordinary, wonderful way of prayer:

> *Lord of life, we thank You that You have the sovereign power to pick up broken lives and turn them into trophies of grace. We here offer You our lives. We confess that Christ lived the life we can never live and that His death paid the penalty for our sins and that His rising again from the dead secured our eternal life. Forgive us for unbelief and work a work of grace in our lives. Show us Your wonder.*
>
> *Lord of life, use us to speak to others about You out of the overflowing experience of Your wonder in our own lives. Lord, teach us to believe again. Lord, relieve us of a small faith in a small god and awaken us to the old, old story of Jesus and His love. And remind us, each day of our lives, each moment of failure, each time we catch ourselves living out of pride rather than Your work of grace, each time hope seems a distant memory, that what God starts, God completes.*
>
> *In the Name of Jesus Christ our Lord, we pray. Amen.*

Postscript

Chancellor of Reformed Theological Seminary

Since the first edition of *What God Starts, God Completes,* God has blessed the encouraging invitation of William MacKenzie many times over, 'Mike, I believe that your story will be of help to others.' Thank you William for encouraging me to write this 'testimony,' for it is not a biography as such, but a statement of faith with flesh on it. Many have come to Christ and even more have recommitted their lives to Jesus Christ. Thus, the book comes to a third printing as I enter into the Office of the Chancellor of Reformed Theological Seminary. This is fitting, since, now, God is writing another chapter in my life, just as He continues to write the stories of each of our lives. As Ben Haden used to say, 'What a Christ!' Thus, I pray that this edition shall continue to be a faithful witness to the God who uses broken people to accomplish His redemptive purposes in the world.

I have chosen to retain the postscript to the second edition as it tells the story of how I transitioned from the local pastorate to leading a great seminary like RTS. It was and is all of God.

* * *

A tree. A dream. And the courage to move forward. That is what comes to me now as I sit down to write this postscript to this third edition of What God Starts, God Completes. Let me explain.

While I was completing *What God Starts, God Completes,* I accepted the call to become President of Reformed Theological Seminary, Charlotte, North Carolina.

I had entered a period of reflection on my future as senior minister at the church I loved so much, First Presbyterian Church of Chattanooga. The reasons for that decision to think and pray about that need not be repeated here. But there comes times, in the life of a shepherd of Christ's flock, where one begins to look at the sheep, look at himself, and look to God. And questions come. 'Would another man be better to lead the flock further into the pastures of God? Have I led them out of the place where they were and brought them to a new place only to relinquish my staff to another? Are you doing this to call me to follow you to a new pasture myself, for I, too, am your lamb?' All of these thoughts came to me. And I declared to several of our leaders that I was intentionally entering a self-imposed season of prayer to seek the Lord's leading. I had no answers, no preconceived directions, and as far as I could tell from my human condition, admittedly prone to self-deception, I was waiting on God from a 'pure heart' if I am allowed to put it that way.

Three days later Reformed Theological Seminary entered my life. Though an emissary of Dr. Ric Cannada, Chancellor and CEO of the RTS institution, I was invited to reflect with them on God's will for my relationship with them. In another couple of days, Dr. Cannada called me personally. My wife and I were both honored but hesitant and uncommitted. I had declined such invitations several times before. But I had never come to this point at my church. I had never allowed myself, for good reason, to reflect on any other identity but the one I had. So this came at exactly the time when I was ready to enter a season of reflection. The events that followed were nothing short of a gift from God. RTS contracted with some other disciples of the Lord, at People Management out of Nashville, who focused on helping others discover their motivational patterns in vocation. 'What makes you tick' and 'What turns you on' in ministry was the idea. I remember distinctly, now, flying across the Atlantic at 35,000 feet in the air, on my way to preach at Cambridge in the Easter cycle of 2007, working through a rather long questionnaire. During that time I went from my childhood to First Presbyterian, Chattanooga, and prayed, reflected and recalled things I had not thought of for a long time: starting a football team, with a friend, that evolved into a high school program that still exists; winning awards with a stock breed calf that I raised from birth to blue ribbons; art exhibitions, sales territories started, churches planted, dreams and visions cast. The folks at People Management prayed with me, talked with me, and indeed, in answer to the leading of the Spirit, led me through a long period of reflection. At the end, I began to see that the open door before me at Reformed Seminary might, indeed, be one, which had been opened by the hand of God. No one took that for granted however. Especially Mae. So we intentionally set up a series of 'doors' for lack of a better term. We felt that each of these metaphorical passageways would need to open in order to even consider answering this call. Each of them, and there were about a dozen, opened. One of those doors was submitting to the faculty, which I could be called to lead. And so I underwent faculty interviews. And once again another door flung open. I was called to become Professor of Practical Theology as well as President of RTS Charlotte. That was an important watershed event in discerning the lord's call. But it was not the decisive one. For I had to understand that the Lord was 'extruding' me (Francis Schaeffer's wonderful description of what must happen in this process) from First Presbyterian, Chattanooga, in order to follow this call. Without going into it, both Mae and I understood that what God was doing in our lives was related to what He wanted to do with our beautiful flock at First Presbyterian. And so a call came together. But let me digress to an event that happened earlier in the process of being called to RTS that came up again as I had to disclose this call to our session and our congregation.

We agreed to visit the campus earlier. While there, I had one of those existential moments that defies logic and goes right to the heart and soul. As my family and I strolled through the picturesque campus of RTS Charlotte, I paused and looked out at this certain tree. It was as if I saw the dream of what could be under the shade of that tree. I asked my family to pause, too. I pointed to the tree and said, 'You know, I think I can see myself under that tree with a brown bag lunch, a Bible, some students gathered around and talking about preaching the Kingdom of God.' They smiled. We moved on. Sometime later, after all of those doors opened, and the Lord confirmed that I was released to follow this call, I was heading down the mountain, where we lived, to tell our session that I had accepted the call to become president of RTS. I found it extraordinarily difficult to face this moment. Love and common life work together in the pastoral ministry to create sacred bonds that are not easily broken, and in a way, never fully undone. My 13 year-old-son saw my tears.

> *'Dad, just remember the tree. Remember the tree where you said that you would teach future pastors. Remember the tree and go and tell them. Tell them we are not leaving…we are following.'*

I have never wiser words. And my son's courage and vision reminded me of how we were being led, once again, to follow the Lord, this time to a tree, the metaphor in our experience for leading a 'seed bed' (the meaning of seminary) of pastor-scholars raising up other pastors and missionaries in fulfillment of 2 Timothy 2:2:

> 'And what you have heard from me in the presence of many witnesses entrust to faithful men who will be able to teach others also' (2 Tim. 2:2).

And so we followed. And like any pastor who loves his flock and must entrust them to the one true Shepherd, we wept even as we looked towards God's call. But since coming we have learned again the truth of this book, of truth that I pray you will know in your own life: that what God starts, God completes. In 2009 I was selected to receive the James M. Baird Jr. Chair of Pastoral Theology. In September, 2010, I was called to follow my friend Dr. Cannada to become the Chancellor of Reformed Theological Seminary. What an honor to stand in the line with such faithful men of God as Sam Patterson, Luder Whitlock and Ric Cannada. What a humbling experience to labor with our campus presidents, faculty, staff, students from over 60 denominations, and over 11,000 alumni serving God in over 70 countries.

Thus now another leg of the journey continues. *What God Starts, God Completes*. Lord has mercy. Christ has mercy.

Michael A. Milton, Ph.D. (University of Wales)
Chancellor and Chief Executive Officer
The James M. Baird Jr. Chair of Pastoral Theology
Reformed Theological Seminary

Reformed Theological Seminary

Founded in 1966, RTS was established to provide solid pastoral training grounded in a commitment to the authority of Scripture and the theological understanding of the Bible found in the Westminster Confession of Faith and the larger and shorter catechisms. Independently governed by a board of trustees, RTS serves students from over 60 evangelical denominations and churches. The seminary does not accept any government funding to assure its fidelity to its founding principles.

The first campus was located in Jackson, Mississippi, with additional campuses being established in later years in Orlando Florida; Charlotte, North Carolina; Atlanta, Georgia; and Washington D.C. In addition to these campuses, RTS now has extension campuses in Memphis, Tennessee; Houston, Texas and we offer an online master's degree from our Virtual campus that serves students in countries throughout the world.

RTS is known for its academic rigor, effective pastoral preparation, commitment to missions and its flexible delivery systems and program accessibility. A bounty of information about our campuses and degree programs is available online at www.rts.edu. Free course lectures and other learning resources are available to all and can be downloaded at http://itunes.rts.edu.

Financial support by individuals and churches is not only appreciatively accepted, but is necessary for the ongoing ministry of the seminary.

Donations may be sent to:

RTS, 5422 Clinton Blvd, Jackson, Mississippi, 39209

Other Works

by

Dr Michael A. Milton

Dr. Milton's Books

A Commentary on Leviticus—(Christian Focus, awaiting publication)

A Commentary on Jeremiah—(EP Press, awaiting publication)

A New Pastoral Theology for the Church Today – (Christian Focus, awaiting publication)

Sacred Assembly: 15 Biblical Steps to Renew your Church (P&R Publications, awaiting publication)

Lord, I Want to Follow Your Call: Preparing for Pastoral Ministry – (EP Press, awaiting publication, 2012)

What is the Doctrine of Adoption? (P & R Publishing 2012)

Songs in the Night: How God Transforms our Pain to Praise (P & R Publishing, 2011)

Hit By Friendly Fire: What to do When Christians Hurt You – (2nd Edition, EP Press, 2011)

Small Things, Big Things: Inspiring Stories of Everyday Grace (P & R Publishing 2009)

What is the Doctrine of the Perseverance of the Saints? (P & R Publishing, 2009)

Cooperation Without Compromise: Faithful Gospel Witness in a Pluralistic Setting – (Wipf & Stock Publishers, 2007)

Oh, the Deep, Deep Love of Jesus: Expository Messages from John 17 – (Wipf & Stock Publishers, 2007)

Following Ben: Expository Preaching as the Power for Frail Followers of Pulpit Giants (Wipf & Stock Publishers, 2004)

Giving as an Act of Worship – (Wipf & Stock Publishers, 2002)

Authentic Christianity and the Life of Freedom: Expository Messages from Galatians – (Wipf & Stock Publishers, May 2005)

The Demands of Discipleship: Expository Messages from Daniel – (Wipf & Stock Publishers, 2005)

Leaving a Career to Follow a Call: A Vocational Guide to the Ordained Ministry—(Wipf & Stock Publishers, 2000)

Dr. Milton's CD's

When Heaven Came Down: Original Christmas Songs by Michael Milton (Music for Missions, 2012)

Through the Open Door (Music for Missions, 2010)

Follow Your Call (Music for Missions, 2008)

He Shall Restore (Music for Missions, 2005)

Here are some other biographies available from Christian Focus...

ISBN 978-1-85792-918-8

Flight Path

A biography of Frank Barker, Jr.

Janie Buck and Mary Lou Davis

Frank Barker:

A Fighter Pilot
A Pastor
A Founder of Briarwood Presbyterian Church
A Servant of Christ.

An interesting book that tells a fascinating life-story, *Flight Path* was an enjoyable read and one I am glad to recommend.

Tim Challies ~ Blogger at www.challies.com

I do not believe that anyone can read this exciting and moving story of lives lived for the kingdom of God without becoming a better person through the experience.

D. James Kennedy ~ Late Pastor of Coral Ridge Presbyterian Church, Fort Lauderdale, Florida

This is the page-turning story of one of the most remarkable ministers of the Gospel I have ever known. I wish that every young minister could spend a year under the tutelage of Frank Barker. A great read about a mighty man of God!

Timothy George ~ Dean of Beeson Divinity School, Samford University, Birmingham, Alabama

The story of Frank Barker is an amazing account of how God uses the faithful and the humble. In a marvelous way Christ sought him, saved him, and made him an effective instrument for the building up of the church. What a remarkable and encouraging legacy!

John MacArthur ~ Pastor, Grace Community Church, Sun Valley, California

ISBN 978-1-84550-542-4

Awakening

The Life and Ministry of Robert Murray McCheyne

David Robertson

'Was Mccheyne for real?'; 'Was he just famous because he died so young?'; 'Does he have anything to teach us today?'

In this book, David Robertson, the present-day minister of McCheyne's church, St Peter's in Dundee, Scotland, seeks to answer these and other questions. Through the use of published sermons, private papers and historical material, this contemporary devotional biography traces McCheyne's life and influence from his upbringing, conversion and training for the ministry to the revival that occurred in St Peter's in 1839 and his early death. The contemporary relevance of McCheyne for today's church is demonstrated and the glory of God is seen in this wonderful story of what He can do with one 'consecrated sinner'.

The freshest presentation of McCheyne available.

Ligon Duncan ~ Senior Minister, First Presbyterian Church, Jackson, Mississippi

Having used Robert Murray McCheyne's 1842 Bible Reading Calendar for many years, and having admired his hunger for holiness, I am very glad that David Robertson has written this new biography.

John Stott ~ Rector Emeritus, All Souls Church, Langham Place, London

...a fine and fresh account of a great and godly minister of the gospel. David Robertson gives us new insight into McCheyne's personal life, and his preparation for preaching, his deep social concern and his absolute devotion to the glory of God as the ultimate motive of everything he did.

Eric Alexander ~ Conference speaker and formerly minister St George's Tron, Glasgow for 20 years.

Christian Focus Publications
publishes books for all ages

Our mission statement –

STAYING FAITHFUL
In dependence upon God we seek to impact the world through literature faithful to His infallible Word, the Bible. Our aim is to ensure that the Lord Jesus Christ is presented as the only hope to obtain forgiveness of sin, live a useful life and look forward to heaven with Him.

REACHING OUT
Christ's last command requires us to reach out to our world with His gospel. We seek to help fulfil that by publishing books that point people towards Jesus and help them develop a Christ-like maturity. We aim to equip all levels of readers for life, work, ministry and mission.

Books in our adult range are published in three imprints:

Christian Focus contains popular works including biographies, commentaries, basic doctrine and Christian living. Our children's books are also published in this imprint.

Mentor focuses on books written at a level suitable for Bible College and seminary students, pastors, and other serious readers. The imprint includes commentaries, doctrinal studies, examination of current issues and church history.

Christian Heritage contains classic writings from the past.

Christian Focus Publications Ltd,
Geanies House, Fearn, Ross-shire,
IV20 1TW, Scotland, United Kingdom.
www.christianfocus.com